BODIE

THE GOLDEN YEARS

A Historical Narrative

JUDY DANIEL

Bodie: Photo by Author.

ISBN: 0-615-57427-0
ISBN-13: 978-0-615-57427-1

BODIE

THE GOLDEN YEARS

INTRODUCTION

It is a bitter cold and windy dawn. Carefully turn up the lantern and stoke the stove to bring a touch of warmth to your cold fingers. The sun is a mere glow, lazily abed behind the rolling sagebrush hills.

Take a visual journey with me back to California's golden days. Let go of today's complications and open your eyes to peer through this window and view the daily life of residents long-departed.

The location is Mono County, California, a high-altitude country straddling the Sierra Nevada Mountains, famous for magnificent glacial granite cliffs and lush forests of pine, aspen, and wildflowers.

The specific place is the mining camp of Bodie, populated by real people from the 1860s through the 1940s, and with ghostly shadow people who can be glimpsed even today, if only just beyond your vision.

The frantic hunt for gold is the reason this mountainous, inhospitable region of tumbleweed territory became a town. The people who made it their home are legendary for their delight in the ridiculous difficulty of settling here.

Ordinary people leave a faint footprint, but their hopes and dreams create a more lasting memory. This is a story of home and family. And although the narrative is my own, the characters are real—Let me now introduce them.

Helen Anne Kernohan resided in Bodie in 1863 with her parents-

Elizabeth Anne Kernohan, one of the first female residents of the town, and Bodie mining pioneer Robert Kernohan. Elizabeth lived in and around Bodie for over forty years.

Margaret and Alice Beck, mother and daughter, resided in Bodie for the majority of their lives. They were wife and daughter of a miner, Joseph Beck, a native of Ireland who for thirty-five years worked the Standard Mine and lived in Bodie.

Pearl Chung is a make-believe resident of Bodie's quite real and infamous Chinatown, on King Street. Pearl is a product of my fascination with the Chinese families who made a valuable contribution to Bodie and California, though rendered invisible by the sifted emotions of history.

Suzy Bill is my artistic rendering of the Mono Lake Kuzedika native people. A photograph of Suzy as a young woman in 1904, standing with the serene Yosemite Falls as a backdrop, has memorialized her as lovely and thoughtful. She stands as testimony to the native culture that shaped all of Mono County, as well as playing an intimate role in Bodie family life. Suzy lived with one foot in the past, where her people lived a pastoral existence in the bountiful foothills of the Eastern Sierra Mountains, and the other sadly mired in the reality of gold rush California. Her people were forced to accept, adapt to, or face certain annihilation from the influx of pioneers, miners, churches, and tea parties. But the path of the Mono Lake native peoples is a testimony to their determination to preserve their culture and create an impact on history.

Lastly we meet Jessie Delilah "Doll" Cain, daughter of the golden age of California, the 1880s through the 1900s. Jessie Delilah is a delightful character, who is thought to be born in Bodie and most definitely lived there for many years with her parents, Martha Delilah and James Stuart Cain. The golden age molded Jessie into a truly modern woman, with the benefit of a well-balanced home life in an established, law-abiding town. Bodie provided her with an education and the security of cultural enrichment. "Doll" enjoyed the quintessential childhood we all hope for, with a lively imagination, time for mischief and freedom, and a loving family to balance the path to adulthood.

Robert E. Stewart, author and Nevada historian, edited this book. Kent G. Stoddard, president of the Mono County Historical Society, generously shared historical photographs from the museum's collections.

This book is dedicated to Sierra, our Queensland/golden lab, who inspired us every day to investigate the trail through sagebrush and snow and helped us see and smell the world beyond our own.

Stroller from Bodie-Mono County Schoolhouse Museum-Author's photo

CHAPTER ONE:
THE LIFE OF A VIRTUOUS GIRL

A Case of Bumping

*Yesterday Justice Peterson was obliged to listen to a tale of woe which originated in the lower dance house. Amelia Torres had a Spanish dame named Rosa arrested for battery. Amelia complained that while she was engaged in dancing a waltz Rosa and her partner bumped against her, much to her annoyance, and when she remonstrated, the bumper slapped her in the face and at the same time used language which shocked her moral sensibilities. Several witnesses were on the stand including the defendant and they swore positively that they witnessed no such proceedings. The plaintiff is a girl who earns a living for herself and mother by dancing in public places, is a modest unassuming senorita, and evidently told the truth when she felt injured and shocked by the unladylike bumping of her assailant. But the jury felt it a solemn duty to acquit the defendant. **The life of a virtuous dance-hall girl is not a merry one, and there are trials to be borne which should be accepted as a penalty for leading such a life, and nothing more.***

– Bodie Free Press 1879

1

My name is Helen Anne.

I was one year of age when my mother, Elizabeth Butler Kernohan, moved to the mining camp of Bodie in the High Sierras with my father, Robert William Kernohan.

I was born in Placerville, California in 1862, and like so many others, my family was following the flashes of golden excitement that was making and breaking boomtowns across the mountains and valleys of California.

My mother always treated me like her gold mine. Mother was a strong-willed, no-nonsense woman, and I would always be her only child, which you other "only babes" know is a great responsibility. I had to be always aware that I was living up to Mother's expectations.

Father was a man on the move, as they used to say. Mother said he was born in Ireland about 1835, and earned his passage to the Americas as a young man filled with golden dreams. Father was well-known in Carson City over in Nevada, and had made partnerships in previous mining prospecting ventures with my mother's brothers, Wilson and Benjamin Butler.

My mother was born in rural Wisconsin in 1843. At eighteen, my mother came to the West with her brothers, which she always referred to as her "great walk." It was 1860, and her brothers were determined to find gold and make their fortunes. Mother was determined to make sure that they were well fed and had their clothes mended, and that they remembered to be true to the family.

Back home were churches, schools, and settled ways of marriage and childrearing—mother was out of the ordinary, though inside she was always the girl from Wisconsin. Midwestern morals were bred into her so deeply, it was going to take more than the wilds of California to have her put them aside.

Carson City, Nevada was full of talk of gold, and the mighty Comstock was in full swing, pumping out precious metals. But the Butlers were Johnnie-come-almost-too-late to these events. Most of the easy pickings of the early panning days had been exhausted by the hordes of men who came in the 1850s. The precious minerals now were buried deeper than the placer gold washing down California's waterways, and the pick and shovel was now the most valued friend of the gold seekers. The Comstock was deep-shaft mining. It required great capital, financing, and large organized masses of miners, carpenters, blacksmiths, and engineers to delve into hundreds of feet of rock.

For my uncles, the Comstock no longer held the opportunity to make a big strike—all the paying claims were taken. The only work was for common laborers paid at three dollars a day. The boys had not come all this distance for work that was no better than back home.

When crowds of men gathered, the talk was always pointing elsewhere—to nearby Gold Hill and Silver City; over the Sierra to Nevada City and Placerville. Then

> Whatever you think proper to grant a child, let it be granted at the first word, without entreaty or prayer, and above all, without making conditions. Grant with pleasure, refuse with reluctance, but let your refusal be irrevocable; let the word "no" when said, and only said when absolutely necessary, be that. Be gentle, but firm, and love and respect will follow.
>
> –The Alpine Chronicle January 4, 1879

Woman is man's help mate, and that does not mean only woman as wife. Happily many women quite understand it. Many girls know their duty is not ended when they make themselves pretty, so that in time some other man will take them off their father's hands and give them more than he can. I think that amongst those I know who are thus helpful, there are more who are really womanly and sweet, who are more truly what women should be at home, than amongst those who, without a thought of helping anybody, regard all men simply as makers of money, on whose shoulders all care and responsibility may be thrown.

–Mary Kyle Dallas, The Alpine Chronicle 1879.

In the fall of 1860 a new name, Esmeralda District, was added. My uncles were right in the thick of all the speculation. And among themselves they spoke more and more of moving on.

The marriage of Robert Kernohan to my mother, Elizabeth Butler, brought the man who would be my father into the group. Now it was time to move on, and they all lit out for Placerville. It was in that mountain settlement that I was born.

In the winter of 1860-61, a town named Aurora was laid out in the Esmeralda Mining District, located along the border between California and the Territory of Nevada, some seventy miles southeast of Carson City. Placerville had been a disappointment; Aurora held real promise. Rumors were flying about that place where boulders heavy with gold and silver had been found right on the surface! Chasing that dream of wealth that would cause our family a lifetime of adventures and misadventures, they—we—headed for Aurora.

Mother's family was bred with strong ties of loyalty to one another. Originally from Potosi county Wisconsin, Grandfather was born after the Butlers had moved to Posey, Indiana on January 5, 1809. Grandfather married Anne Coats in Posey. The family was strong pioneer stock–grandfather was a blacksmith by trade. In that day, a blacksmith was strong, and patient enough to manhandle raw iron into useful, often beautiful, items. He and Anne were blessed with many children–Daniel, Anna, Wilson, Benjamin, Elizabeth (my mother), Elizah, Martha, Sarah, and Marietta.

As I said before the Gold Fever swept across the land; the brothers Wilson and Benjamin, joined the rest of America and jumped off the edge of the settled lands to make their way by ox- drawn wagon train to the California. My Mother was unmarried at this time, and so she determined to join the boys on their adventure, as cook, laundress, and mother to the brothers.

Perhaps this long trek was the glue that bonded these three for the remaining years of their lives-for they would live within a county's walk of each other for their entire lives. For my mother this meant bidding adieu to Father when he picked up stakes in California and moved to Washington State for a new venture.

Mother never spoke ill of her husband Robert after he left, and later on even allowed me to travel to Washington to sit with Father near the end of his life. But Elizabeth made her stand in Mono County, and there she remained, outliving three husbands in her stubbornness, but always keeping her head high. No one could ever fault her warm, powerful moral character.

My mother had quickly learned a powerful lesson-the men may dig the earth for golden riches, but all men must eat and all men must sleep, and there lies a fortune for the woman who can rustle up a decent meal and launder the bedding for men too tired from the day's labor. Perhaps mother started as nursemaid to her brothers, but for sure marriage never dented her ability to hire herself out as cook, innkeeper and jack of all trades hospitable.

In 1863, my parents and I moved from the relatively civilized town of Aurora to father's better prospects in the Bodie Bluffs camp. For the camp of Bodie, you see, was not much of a place for ladies to visit, let alone to set up a home. Mother and Father had claim to one of the hastily- built miner's cabins. At least this was a step above a lean-to on the hillside or one of the canvas tents some single miners were occupying.

These "cabins" were typically one large room with an open hearth to one side

Frontier Kitchens

On the frontier, and in early Bodie, the term "kitchen" must be taken in historical context. For many frontier families, the fireplace was the primary means of cooking...which necessitated the use of a system of hooks and brackets over the flames, from which pots and kettles were hung...settlers used Dutch ovens, half-cylinders of tin which sat in front of the fire and cooked meats. When cook stoves were available, they still had to be continuously supplied with fuel, and banked at night, and tended to belch ashes into the air, and fill the home with noxious fumes.

Cookstoves did not come with thermostats, so temperatures and baking times were all guesswork. Recipes were based upon experience, and lack of store-bought supplies led to constant substitutions.

Meals were high in fat and very salty—but families were working from dawn until dusk, often in freezing weather, and these diets were welcome.

Residents of Bodie could not step off to the local grocery store, and the bulk of the diet was harvested or gathered from the wilderness that surrounded them. Families that could, grew their own fruits and vegetables in summer, and preserved every bit they did not consume for the long winters, when scurvy was a real threat.

The most common method of preserving was to lay out the produce on clean cloth and dry it, even the meat from a good hunt. Meats had to be eaten almost immediately, so women would roast or par-roast it to make it last. Often the dried meat was heavily salted to keep it from rotting. In 1858, the Mason jar with its rubber ring and wire ring was introduced, but many pioneer women did not have access to this convenience. Storage containers for dried fruits or vegetables had to be creative and available, and it was common to rinse kerosene tins to re-use as containers for the family foods.

Cooking stoves had to be hauled great distances to the frontier cabin, and often took the skilled services of a tinsmith to assemble so that they did not burn down the house. Early models were heavy, small, and required quite a bit of bending over to keep fired up.

A Bodie kitchen (Photo by Author)

where cooking was done over an open fire. Often beds built around the sides of the room were sheltered by a drawn curtain for sleeping. Often several single miners would bunk together and one fellow would be voted cook and another housekeeper.

As you might imagine, the men could never match my mother for sweeping, much less for baking a good biscuit to dip in the stew.

I can always see Mother in my memory, setting the supper table for Father and me, as well as several paying customers as long as the supplies held out. Often the miners would pay Mother with flour, sugar, fresh trout, jackass rabbits, or even venison from their hunting.

Supplies were hard to procure. There were no stores. Father had to rent or borrow a team and wagon and go fifteen miles back to Aurora, or perhaps to Monoville north of Mono Lake. There, he would buy flour, baking powder and soda, beans, sugar, and of course coffee and tea. If Father could not be bothered because of his mining work, Mother would trade services (laundering, fresh baked pies, a good cabin cleaning) with some fellow who might be going to get supplies.

Laundry itself was an all-day affair. Mother had to carry in water to fill the big kettle and bring it to a boil on the kitchen stove, then pour successive buckets over the clothes in the big metal bathing tub. She made the soap by hand before any laundering could begin. After the clothing was scrubbed and rinsed as best Mother could manage, she hung it out-of-doors in good weather (rare in Bodie) or inside our tiny living space when the weather was bad (most of the winter). You cannot but agree that laundry day always came too soon for Mother!

You had best believe Mother could take in about all the laundry anyone could want, as the menfolk seemed desire this service highly. But it was very hard work, and the Piute women would do it for a handout—much less than it was worth to Mother, who on most occasions could make a better profit with her cooking and baking skills.

Of course, Uncle Ben and Auntie Mary Elizabeth still lived in Aurora. Auntie did not think highly of the Bodie accommodations, and there were no schools set up for her soon-to-be-born children. In his comings and goings, Uncle Ben often brought the supplies our family needed.

So perhaps you can understand how Mother got her strong temperament. If Father could not get it done, mother could. Mother started earning her own spending money, and in the lean times, Father had to swallow his Irish pride while Mother kept the family afloat.

Life in Bodie when I was a child remains for me a memory of our little cabin, which was my whole world during the long months when the snow closed off the outdoors. As a small child I was never out of my mother's sight, and her work in the home kept her busy from sunup to the darkness of night.

Mother always made our times cheerful when we were alone, for Father was often gone for many nights, attending to his business. Mother was always busy making our cabin clean, if not lavish, and warm with the ever-burning fire at the cookstove. Mother sewed all my clothes by hand, and she would pore over pictures of ladies' fashions, copying patterns to make my small dresses. So I had several play dresses of gingham, and over-aprons to protect my clothes and cut down on daily laundering. For my fifth birthday, Mother surprised me with a fancy dress, just like grown-up ladies wore in Aurora.

Soap Making

First the fat for the project was to be obtained, usually from cutting off the fat of an animal butchered for the meals. This fat was finely chopped, and cooked down in a large pot until the cracklings were floating in the boiling fat. The fat was drained off into pails stored in a cool place, such as a root cellar, to be used later to be used in the cooking of pies or other items. The crackling were put back into the large pot, and heated again, adding lye, sprinkling the crystals on top of the cracklings. Then water was added, and all was stirred until the cracklings disappeared, continuing to boil and stir, and using a long wooden spoon it was poured out on a testing plate and was done when this was the consistency of soft cheese, usually about the time it was leaving a creamy layer on the stirring stick-spoon. Now it was poured into a small tub about 4 inches deep, and would set up over the course of about 24 hours. The tub was next turned over and it was cut into smaller pieces, and set on a drying board for several days. It could then be stored in a box and was ready to use.

—*Soap Making-The Way We Used to Do It* by Mabel Mertz

Mother had Father take us all the way to Aurora so I could pose for a portrait in that dress. Goodness, I rarely got to even wear it, but Mother was always proud to show the little photo to all that wanted to look.

I remember Bodie as my first true home, for Mother determined that Father's wandering days must take second place to taking care of the two of us. And for a time, as Father was doing fairly well in his mining ventures, we did stay put.

Mother's brother Wilson set up blacksmithing, and brother Ben determined to make a go as a cordwood supplier for the fuel-greedy mines. Their steam engines were consuming miles of firewood. Timber to construct the supports in the diggings was also in demand. Father formed a mining cooperative with Mr. Olsen, late of Aurora. It was then that our little family took over a small cabin on Browne Street, named after the arrival of the *Harper's Monthly* writer Mr. J. Ross Browne, though several years later, the importance of his visit faded and the dirt lane was renamed Green Street. Our new cabin had mud walls and a window with a shutter but no glass. It soon had a real iron wood cookstove, which Mother had her brother Wilson haul all the way from Aurora. Father was overwhelmed by its complicated construction, but Uncle Wilson had studied blacksmithing under his father Daniel Butler, and so soon had it set up and working fine. We had a small wooden table, with an assortment of stools and pine chairs set about it. Once the young miners got a whiff of

Mother's baked goods, the chairs seemed to always be occupied by a friendly crowd. At first, they didn't actually pay Mother for vittles, breads, biscuits, and whatever else she had made up. But soon items began to come to us—like the fine rocker in which Mother would sit while she sewed my little dresses, and a mirror and hope chest with some warm blankets. After a while, when father would allow it, miners would just pick up items and leave some gold or silver bounty that Mother would save for a rainy day.

Soon our cabin had real glass in the window frames. A wood floor came next, and a worn carpet came from the cabin up the way when its occupants left for better prospects.

It is true Bodie was not much of a town. No matter how glorious the future that was to come, in the 1860s there were still few women for Mother to converse with, excluding the Paiute women and some other ladies Mother always told me not to notice if per chance we did see them in the light of day.

I was indeed very special, being the first proper white child, and a female, to actually live in the settlement. We had frequent visits from Uncle Ben and his wife, and they had several children in good time, but they did not actually live in Bodie. I guess these other children thought I was a bit spoiled. And it is true that when the miners managed to procure their supplies, somehow a bit of hard candy would fall into my happy hands.

Even though Mother was more interested in obtaining a small reader for me to supplement our Bible, she never turned down the cotton cloth that the gentle miners felt would make a better dress for me than a shirt for themselves. I know that even though we were comfortable in our little cabin, mother truly missed other womenfolk. Mother would write long and frequent letters back home to Wisconsin to her mother and sisters.

Women's Work

California began its gold rush days as an almost-exclusively male-dominated adventure. In the absence of women to do "women's work," such as cooking, cleaning, laundering, sewing, ironing, canning, and soap making, the value placed upon procuring these services greatly increased. The few married women who came in the first waves across the frontier to California found that there was profit in baking pies, setting up clean lodging, or nursing the sick. Married women were often surprised to be earning more than their husbands, for as these often incompetent amateurs floundered in the increasingly-complex technological demands of mining gold, women thrived doing what their mothers had taught them as small girls—taking care of the men.

In the California of the 1850s and 1860s, ladies did not dare live alone or work in bars, saloons, or dance halls. Young women lived with parents, brothers, and even sisters until they married. A wife had to first do her duty to her husband, whether he lived in the cities of the East, traveled west by ship or wagon train, or decided to settle miles from nowhere in a rough mining camp.

Once the household's daily chores were done, women were free and often encouraged, in this new, uncivilized California, to open small businesses and make money to contribute to the men's mining endeavors. As long as the lady kept it quiet and did not threaten the real business of the men, she was allowed to earn whatever money she could in polite trades—cooking, especially baked goods, dressmaking, housecleaning, or book-learning.

Fancy girls or so-called "gay" women danced or worked the saloons. Still worse were the "sporting" girls (prostitutes). Both were looked down upon, often never able to regain the company of virtuous ladies. It was the virtuous ladies themselves, rather than the men, who did not forgive the fallen doves, perhaps because life was so very tough for women in the mining camps and towns, isolated from their mothers, their churches, and their teatimes. Something had to toughen up in these women, and they held themselves to the highest possible moral standard. No one could be more severe than a young woman earning bottom dollar taking in sewing toward a fellow female making a fast fistful of cash consorting with men. Morality became all women could hold onto from their lives in the East, and it became the cornerstone of the new gold towns. Churches were built, women's aid societies were formed, books were dusted off and schools were funded.

Lo and behold! Her prayers were answered when Marietta, Mother's younger sister, accompanied Grandfather Daniel on one of his three cross-country journeys to visit his children.

The only ones happier than Mother to see her lively sister Marietta were the single gentlemen of the area! To sit and visit with Mother was a treat to the lonely miners, but the chance to sit with the lovely, single Marietta caused our little circle of friends to expand greatly.

Marietta was courted by Mr. Rodger Horner. It seems that they made the perfect pair, and while Marietta had planned to just visit, she accepted Mr. Horner's offer of marriage. For her, moving back to Wisconsin was delayed.

You can imagine that our little camp fairly buzzed with excitement—a wedding was planned for mid-January. I do not know who was the most excited, the blissful couple or the guests. The entire respectable community of Bodie, and several close friends, uncles, aunts, and cousins from Aurora planned to attend. Mother added a bit of ruffle to my old dress, and Marietta purchased some fine satin ribbon for my hair. It was a memorable time for us all.

In the middle of the long, cold, dark days of the Bodie winter, a party formed to welcome Reverend J. M. Dudleston from Aurora. He officiated at the solemn and happy occasion at which Marietta became Mrs. Horner. Mother sat with auntie to sew a bright wedding dress out of fine striped cotton. Mother had saved the cloth from a while back and the finished product was simple, but it was still beyond anything that a young bride in Bodie could wish for. Mother had her new shawl with the fine fringe over her blouse, and her long gown turned her into such a fine lady. Father looked handsome, if uncomfortable, in his only suit. Of course, all the guests were dressed in their Sunday best.

The food was never-ending. Mother had peach preserves, fresh biscuits, and potatoes and real carrots from the Mono Lake farmers. A whole beef was prepped and brought by my uncles, Ben and Wilson.

After the ceremony, the music began. Father and the brothers constructed a small platform of timbers from the mining operations to create a makeshift dance floor. Folks came from as far as Aurora, Monoville, and all the ranches in between, and nobody intended to leave early. The miners cleaned up like they were back home and patiently waited their turn to twirl about the few married ladies present. And then all the folks ate and told stories of their golden dreams- tall tales most of them, but with a kernel of truth as well.

Marietta had brought a special item from home, a foot treadle sewing machine, which she mastered and that quickly became a local sensation. Mother and Marietta used the sewing machine to prepare all the tailoring needed for the wedding. The whirling sound of the chattering needle soon created

MARRIAGE SUPERSTITIONS

Since marriage became an institution there have been certain signs and superstitions that have clung to its celebration through all the ages and in all countries. Even today, in the most civilized nations, we have, not entirely rid our minds of these superstitions, and I warrant there is never a bride but indulges in looking for some happy omen. Few people are dauntless enough to marry on Friday, and we have the most unlimited confidence in that old shoe thrown after the newly wedded pair—nearly every bride of to-day wears about her when she is married some trifling thing borrowed from a lady friend, and all know that "Blest is the bride on whom the sun doth shine" and are equally certain.

To change the name and not the letter
Is a change for the worse and not for the better.
The old rhyme that we all heard tells us to marry on-
Monday for wealth
Tuesday for health
Wednesday the best day of all
Thursday for crosses
Friday for losses
Saturday no luck at all.
The Alpine Chronicle, January 4, 1879

Recipe for Nut Cake—Two cups of sugar, one cup of butter, three cups of flour, one cup of cold water, four eggs, three teaspoonfuls of baking powder, two cup-full of kernels of hickory-nuts or white walnuts, carefully picked out, and added last of all.

The Alpine Chronicle, Bodie, December 21, 1878.

Recipe for Indian Griddle Cakes—Beat two eggs light, stir into them one quart sweet milk, one teaspoon salt and enough cornmeal to make a good batter, bake on a soap stone griddle as soon as raised, or on a iron one greased with pork. One spoonful of batter for each cake.

–The Alpine Chronicle, Bodie, December 21, 1878.

Marietta's Wedding Dress
(Photo by Author)
Mono County Historical Society

quite a sensation among the native Paiute squaws, who you can just imagine thought the spinning wheel to be the stuff of magic.

An unexpected result of the introduction Marietta's sewing machine to our lives was the effect it had on our neighbors, the native peoples. For the rest of our days in Bodie, Paiute ladies would appear with their faces full of wonder and curiosity at the back window of the house, pulling bright red cotton and other materials out of their baskets, pointing to the precious machine and humbly offering to trade cleaning and laundering, or whatever they saw needed to be done, in exchange for Marietta to "grind" out a dress for them. You see, by the time I was a child, the Paiute, especially the women, had adopted our style of dress, and had peacefully blended into our small camp. We did not fear any attack from them, although before my time there were Indian Wars in the greater Owens Valley, and lives were lost on both sides. The tribal people of our area took the path of coexistence, and through the loss of their historic hunting grounds supplemented their diets with foods for which they could trade their labor.

Other events kept our happy days going. My mother kept her focus on her responsibilities as the center of the Butler family. Aunt Marietta soon gave birth to a child, and our joy at Matthew Daniel Horner's arrival on April 3, 1869 was shared by all of our neighbors.

You can imagine the reverence of the miners, dirty from a long day's work, stopping by to offer some trivial favor just to be able to shyly take a look at my chubby cousin, the first baby born in Bodie. By and large, the miners were decent men, missing their own faraway families fiercely. Stopping in for the biscuit and stew that my mother would offer gave all the men a bit of home. It was a simple pleasure to bask in the glow of well-spoken womenfolk and the tiny cries of a newborn baby.

Life for Mother was now at a turning point. Raised up a proper young lady, Mother had married my father with all the hopes of any young bride. Her job was to cook, to clean, to bear and mind children—to follow her husband through the good times and quietly suffer through the bad.

But something had changed inside Mother on the long walk from her old home to this unsettled California. Outwardly one would never see it, but a fire had started inside Mother that even she could not put out. She had thoughts and feelings and dreams of her own, separate from Father's.

Father was struggling with his mining ventures, finding it hard to keep food on our table. Other men branched out into other trades and went to mining just part-time to increase their family income. Father did not follow this example.

For Father, it was ever more difficult for him to make a living in the Bodie diggings. The gold was farther and farther inside the earth, and it required getting more and more financial backing to supply the things needed to make a profit. And as always, the talk was of other places where one could stake a claim and find gold.

BUY ONLY
THE
NEW AMERICAN!
It is the only sewing machine which has a
SELF-THREADING SHUTTLE.
It has Self-Setting Needle.
Never breaks the Thread.
Never skips Stitches.
Is the Lightest Running.
The Simplest. The most Durable and in every Respect
THE BEST FAMILY SEWING MACHINE
The "New American" is easily learned, does not get out of
order, and will do more work with less labor than any other
machines. Illustrated Circular furnished on application.
The Alpine Chronicle 1878

The sewing machine was patented by the mechanic Elias Howe Jr. in 1846, featuring a horizontal needle and the lock stitch, which was invented by Walter Hunt in the 1830s. But the sewing machine was not embraced by American women, who hand-sewed the majority of the family clothing and domestic necessities until Isaac Singer introduced his version of the sewing machine with the vertical needle and foot treadle in 1851. Singer was an excellent salesman, moving from town to town demonstrating his machine and offering to give out the sewing machines for a small down payment. By the mid-1860s, the sewing machine was in common use and became part of most households.

—The Sewing Machine and Quilters in the 19th Century.
Kimberly Wulfert, Ph.D.

Wedding Anniversaries. In order to refresh the minds of our readers, we publish the list of wedding celebrations.
Three days, sugar; sixty days, vinegar; first anniversary, iron; fifth, wooden; tenth, tin; fifteenth, crystal; twentieth, china; twenty-fifth, silver; thirtieth, cotton; thirty-fifth, linen; fortieth, woolen; forty-fifth, silk; fiftieth, gold; seventy-fifth, diamond.
The Alpine Chronicle, Bodie, 1878

Father was always the most eager of listeners. It seemed the farther away the place was, the more fantastic the stories became. Father began to spend more time with a far-off look in his eye than at the backbreaking work of the diggings.

One night, when I was supposed to be sleeping, I heard Mother's usually-quiet voice raised up: "I am through with moving myself and child in another oxcart!"

It seems this statement was the final moment of their discussion, and if you had ever met Mother, you would know that she might be soft-spoken, but she had backbone and always meant what she said.

Father just could not make her change her mind, but his pride would not allow him to let Mother have the final say. He would leave, with her or alone. So now our precious home was to be sold, and the meager profit divided. Father might chase off to the next excitement, but he respected Mother and would never be one to run out without a word. With that, he was gone.

Mother held her head high. She was a Butler first, and a wife true. By 1870, Mother and I were set up in the Bishop Creek mining community. Mother had a lodging house venture, with her many acquaintances staking her in this business deal. And of course, the brothers never abandoned their sister.

Father got caught up in a business deal way up in Washington State. In leaving Bodie, he had traded away what would turn out to be the richest gold bonanza that California has ever known.

It was many years later that I saw my Father. It was as a married woman, with several children of my own. Father at this time suffered from tuberculosis, and needed help with the small store he ran. Mother had business in Bodie and could not get away. Still chasing his dreams in Washington, Father eventually let go. Mother honored him as a good man, but remarried as soon as it was proper for her to do so. A decent, hard-working woman was indeed of great value in the West.

Sketch of Elizabeth Kernohan by Author

Personal History

Tracing Elizabeth has been a fine and painstaking task, for our Elizabeth was never a famous woman, just a hard-working and honest person who lived and died a century ago. Partly her history is glossed over by the proper moral tones of her day—did she marry three husbands in legal succession, or was there something else going on?

One can never fault her character; Elizabeth was a dedicated family woman and was never criticized or made the subject of gossip.

We have two sets of sources: the historical memoirs of her descendant Frank Wedertz in his book 'Bodie 1859-1900'; and the records of the United States Federal Censuses of 1860, 1870, 1880, and 1900. The 1890 Census was lost in a great and devastating fire.

The facts found in the Wedertz memoir detail her marriage to Robert Kernohan and the birth of their daughter Helen .

Brothers Ben and Wilson are also mentioned; the latter as Bodie's first blacksmith and longest-term resident when he died in 1896. Wilson operated his shop on the corner of Mill and Mono streets.

Ben is mentioned as a mining partner to Robert Kernohan, as a wood dealer, as the father of two children, and as the husband of "Belle," whom Wedertz states was Bodie's first school teacher, opening their house in 1879 to between ten and forty children. Mr. Wedertz is privy to many details as a family historian, but many others list Bodie's first school teacher as Belle Donnally, not Belle Butler.

Ben Butler, Robert Kernohan, Dan Olsen, and Rodger Horner mined the High Peak area and hauled their ore some distance to the location of their crushing arastra, located on Rough Creek. These gentlemen worked the mines themselves, but it appears Robert Kernohan sold out before 1870, while the others stayed in the game until the big companies came in 1879. Wedertz states Robert died of tuberculosis in Pomeroy, Washington. He does not tell the year.

Wedertz, in his book *Bodie:1859-1900*, says clearly that Elizabeth was married three times, but he only mentions Robert Kernohan as the first and Jesse McGath as the third, omitting the second husband. Almond Huntoon is mentioned as one of the longtime pioneer farmers of Bridgeport and early businessman and dairyman, as well as a "business partner" of Elizabeth in the Booker Flat Hotel venture in Bodie. Wedertz also states that Jesse McGath was a skilled carpenter and built the finest house in Bodie for his wife in 1879—the house that is now known as the Cain House at Green and Park Streets. Jesse McGath originally built on Green Street, but in another location, which remains unclear. Ella Cain mentions that the Cain house had a female ghost, who the Cains believed to be that of the first wife of Jesse, who reportedly died in the upstairs bedroom of that house. It could not have been the ghost of Elizabeth—who died in Bridgeport. Many writers report that Jesse McGath built the finest house in Bodie for Elizabeth—but they did not marry until about 1892 (1900 U.S. Federal Census Records) which also indicates that Elizabeth lived in this house only in the 1890s. In his later work *Mono Diggings,* Wedertz clearly indicates that Almond Huntoon and Elizabeth were married, although the dates of this event are not mentioned.

The 1860 U.S. Federal Census lists Elizabeth Anne Butler as nineteen, living in the Grant, Wisconsin home of her father Daniel and mother Anne. Her brothers are listed as Wilson, Benjamin, and Elizah and her sisters as Martha, Sarah, and Mary.

In the 1870 Federal Census, Elizabeth Kernohan, age twenty-seven, was living in a lodging house in Bishop Creek with her daughter Helen. There is no mention of Robert anywhere in the 1870 Census.

In 1880, there is an Elizabeth Huntoon (forty years old, born in Wisconsin), keeping house for A. Huntoon, a dairy farmer in Bodie, with her eighteen-year-old daughter, Hellen A. Huntoon, with Willie and Harvey Butler, two boys ages twelve and nine. Wedertz names Ben Butler's boys as Will and Harvey.

Wedertz also reports that Almond Huntoon was a business partner of Elizabeth's, fronting the money for the Booker Flat Hotel of Bodie, which Elizabeth "managed."

By 1900, Jesse and Elizabeth McGath (age fifty-nine, and born in Wisconsin) were living in Bridgeport, where Jesse is listed as a laborer, and the Cain family is living in the house Jesse built in Bodie, where Jesse lived with his first wife. Elizabeth married Jesse after the death of Almond and lived with Jesse in the finest house in Bodie for several years. At that time today's Cain House was in another location, most probably on upper Green Street.

Helen Anne married a dairyman, John Merrick Sawyer, on April 6, 1879. Her daughter Lyna May Sawyer was born in Bodie on July 8, 1881.

Helen Anne died on May 26, 1885, in Pomeroy, Washington, where the Sawyer family had moved to manage the store and bar that Robert Kernohan owned. Pomeroy is in a remote area in southeast Washington state.

Helen's children returned to the Bodie area, where Lyna May Sawyer married Lewis F. Wedertz.

Elizabeth lived in Bridgeport until her death in 1912, well into her seventies.

Bodie
(Photo by Author)

CHAPTER TWO:
JACKRABBIT STEW

Jack Rabbit Stew: Cut into pieces, including neck, head (eyes being bored out), lungs, liver and heart; place these pieces in an earthen dish, add one onion (sliced), one teaspoonful of whole pepper, two bayberry leaves, twelve cloves, a little parsley and salt, and allow to stand in a cool place for twenty-four hours. When ready... place in a pot...cover, put on the fire and allow it to simmer till soft...

—W.B. Ayer and Co., 1885

One of the things about Bodie that Mother just did not care for was the lack of a proper school for me to attend. Now, I am not saying that this was a matter of concern to me, but it did upset Mother.

After Father went off to Washington State, Mother became even more determined that I receive a proper education. The opportunity to work at the boarding house in Bishop Creek seemed more attractive to her, as there was a good report that there were several families with school-age children in that camp, and there were plans to form a school in the next term.

It was difficult for mother to leave the closeness of her brothers in Mono County—Marietta and her husband had determined to return to Wisconsin to raise their family among proper schools and churches, and to be close to Grandmother Anne and Grandfather Daniel. Her husband's family was from Wisconsin, and opportunities for him were much greater back home. Once the Bodie adventure showed no hope for quick riches anytime soon, Marietta and her husband needed to find a way to support their growing family. Mother was heartbroken to see Marietta pack up her few possessions and make ready to go back home.

Marietta took me aside that last week and pulled out some little things she wanted me to have: a cloth doll that was so very precious, dressed in a calico gown that was made from my own best dress, with long yarn braids of dark wool, and a ribbon in her pigtails. Oh, I finally had my first real doll—I named her Mary Ann after my auntie that I loved so much.

For Mother, losing Marietta was like a cold bucket of Bodie water thrown right at her. The companionship of a close female relative could not be replaced, and though many, many words would be exchanged through letters every week, this was going to be a great loss for my mother.

I saw Mother cry while washing dishes one morning, something I had never ever seen, and I knew the tears were for family moving away—but I pretended not to see, since Mother was always determined to be the strong one and keep her chin up all the time.

The Bishop Creek settlement was not as far away as Washington, where Father had moved. It was only about eighty miles south. The only means of visiting back and forth would mean several days traveling on a dirt road through some very steep and treacherous areas, so moving to Bishop Creek would actually cut us off from the friendly closeness with the Butler brothers and their wives. The brothers were very upset that Mother was to move away, but the farms and ranches of Bishop Creek had milder winters and hotter summers, and there was fresh farm produce for me to eat. Mother could only think of some way to make life better for me, and could not be swayed from this new opportunity.

Her older brother Wilson had great skill in blacksmithing and could supplement his prospecting ventures with a trade that was always in high demand. Her other brother Ben was the organizer and the talker. He made a good living investing in the wood trade—locating, hauling, and brokering lumber to the wood-hungry mines and miners. Both brothers were loath to have mother move, worrying about all the "what-ifs."

All was for naught when it came to convincing mother not to go. Elizabeth Anne Butler Kernohan had walked across the country to settle this new land. She had cooked over an open flame, done laundry in ice-cold creeks, and slept on prairie-grass beds. All her mementos from home had been tossed out onto the prairies or mountains to lighten the load. Now with father splitting up the family to move north, she just couldn't be scared anymore.

Marriage to father had started out just fine, but when mother could take in more cash from cooking and cleaning than father could earn, the writing was on the wall so to speak. Mother was offered a good business opportunity to be a partner in a lodging house in Bishop Creek. She had independence in her blood now and no husband could change that. So the brothers packed us up, and we saw a new family with high hopes take possession of our old house—mother had tears in her eyes but her head was held high.

Marietta and her baby and husband were setting out for Aurora to catch the stage to Carson City and then make their way to Wisconsin by stage and train. The best road kept us all together moving toward Aurora. From there, we took the tried and true Owens River toll road, that wound out of Aurora and through the easier, more-level desert country east of the great Mono Lake and down toward Benton Springs. At that point we had to make a choice of crossing the Owens River at Benton's Crossing and trying the more rugged and shorter route to Bishop Creek along the way most folks called the Lake Country, or steering to the longer, drier, more desert-like route toward the east, and reaching Bishop Creek that way.

We were planning almost ten days on the road, as I recall, just in case there were any washouts on the Benton toll road, which could happen easily with the flash flooding and thunderstorms of the summer months. These road repairs would take several days to remedy, and we planned to camp out on the way. The brothers looked forward to hunting and fishing as we went to supplement the provisions we picked up in Aurora. And lo! On the second day Ben hooked some beautiful little trout for dinner, much to Wilson's delight. Mother prepared them just fine in her iron skillet in a bit of flour, salt, cornmeal, and lard, and with some camp biscuits and canned peaches we were eating like royalty on holiday.

I loved to sit in camp in the evening, looking off to the great snowy Sierra Mountains as I cradled my new doll Mary Ann and sang lullabies to her, just like mother would do in her happier times. Sometimes, as the wagon struggled down the dusty, rocky road, I would prefer to walk with my mother. We even gathered the violet wild irises and red Indian paintbrush flowers. With a few green reeds, I wove flower wreaths for our new home. It became one of my lasting memories for my uncles, who would spot the wild flowers from the wagon and call to me "Child, there is a batch you haven't gathered yet. There close by that brown rock are white buttons, and mind you look afore you pick, gal!" Ever after Uncle Will would surprise me with a new flower, he would say to me: "Remember our little walk when you were a wee child and you gathered all those flowers for your new home?"

Mother would mostly walk along, steady and keeping both eyes on me. Her face looked happy in a very quiet way, drinking in these moments with her brothers and me, saving the thought of them for a letter to Marietta, and for her own pleasure, when their company, too, would be just a memory as she sat sewing and mending at the end of a day's work.

The road was in good repair for most of our journey, so we made good time. We opted to take the safe route through Benton Springs and then take that eastern route; Mother wanted to do some looking-over of the dry goods store there. She hoped to trade her braided cloth rugs for school shoes for me. I usually wore the moccasins Marietta had traded the Indian women for her sewing machine work in Bodie.

Judy Daniel

Biscuits

Take one quart of flour, three teaspoonfuls of cream of tartar, mix well through the flour, two tablespoons of shortening, one teaspoon of soda, dissolved in warm water, of a sufficient quantity to mold the quart of flour.

The History of Hardtack

(http://www.ken Anderson.net/hardtack)

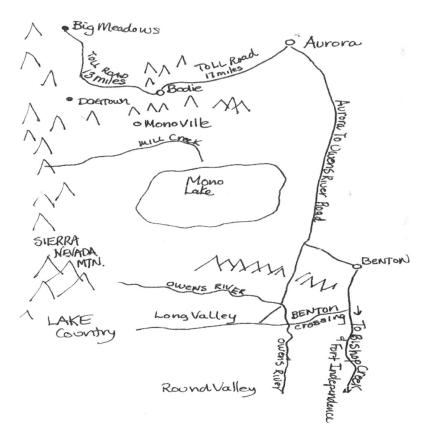

Sketch by Author

35

> *Tell me the tales that to me were so dear*
> *Long, long ago, long, long ago*
> *Sing me the songs I delighted to hear,*
> *Long, long ago, long ago,*
> *Now you are come all my grief is removed,*
> *Let me forget that so long you have roved.*
> *Let me believe that you love as you loved,*
> *Long, long ago, long ago.*
> *Thomas Hayes Bayly (1797-1839)*

It seemed like Bodie and our happy times there were fading the further we went. When we got to Benton Springs, we were all amazed at how that sleepy place was really waking up with merchants and farmers, livestock ranchers, and prospectors shoving elbows to get a look at the goods the town had to offer. Why, last we had heard Benton Springs was just beginning to look like a town. Now it seemed that this place had got the better of Aurora, Monoville, and Bodie. I had never been to the town of Bridgeport at Big Meadows, but Ben said Benton was looking at least as good.

We got some more coffee, flour, salt, some more of those new canned fruits, and some bolts of cotton. Mother promised to make me a new dress with the leftover cloth from the curtains she was planning for our new home. Ben purchased a fine pair of black leather tie-up boots that fit me with some room to spare. He said his niece was going to look like a proper schoolgirl and show what the Butler name was all about. Of course, I did not put them on then, because my old moccasins were already dusty and just fine for traveling.

We finally pulled into Bishop Creek late in the evening. Our first look at the camp was not exactly how Mother's partner in the lodging house had told it. The brothers were not impressed with the rough construction and the generally primitive conditions. But the town seemed to be in a buzz of new hope, the center of ranching and farming enterprises that were making a living for the settlers.

That first morning, Mother got up especially early and swept out the common room and washed the one window, setting about to make the place our home. Mother had time to cook up several eggs she had put by, sliced up and fried some pork, and added some flapjacks. Breakfast made everyone feel a lot more comfortable, especially with Mother's familiar crockery on the table.

The brothers had to hurry back to their own womenfolk and businesses, and there was no time for tears—just a hug all around and a "see you next holiday, hopefully," and they were off.

 The very last thing Uncle Will did was pull out a small wrapped package. He gave it to me and made me promise to listen to Mother, and send word if things did not go as planned. He himself would come as soon as he was able and take us back to his small place at Bodie.

Mother didn't answer this last sally, but told me presents were for later on and that we must get to working right away.

Well, Mother really set to moving us in. She began laundering all the bedding, then moved on to scouring out the cooking area, and didn't stop before trimming up new curtains for the main room, as well as some for our quarters.

Mother told me to watch myself and stay close by, but I sure took that to mean go visiting around to the other families. First off I took count of the children and from infants just born (two of these) and some various small boys, I was pleased to meet the neighbor family that included four brothers of sixteen, twelve, and ten, and two girls of nine and eight. Their mother looked pleased to see me, or just tired from her own, I am not so sure. It was just wonderful to exchange news with these folks, and I gathered there might be about twenty to thirty children all around the camp. It looked like Mother would have her dream—schooling for me.

There was no proper schoolhouse yet, but one of the families was going to

Children's Clothing

Descriptions of children's clothing are based on a study of the portraits from the period, articles and drawings from historical periodicals, and an examination of toys (such as dolls) long protected in museums.

At the Kent State University Museum, the Centuries of Childhood web page (dept.kent.edu/exhibit/kids/kids.HTML) states the prevailing summary: "The history of children's clothing reflects the attitude of adults toward childhood, as, **until** very recently, children had no voice in the matter....children were dressed as miniature adult(s), in garments which limited their physical freedom and imposed societal restrictions on their behavior".

As children moved West with their families, the style of their dress reflected some emancipation from the rigidity of all things back home. Most clothing was sewn by a mother who was also cooking over an open hearth, making her own soap, and skinning the meat for the family meal. Fashion magazines and fashionable dress materials were not available in most frontier locations.

Bolts of demure calico or dark woolens might be purchased if the family was lucky to be in a town and had extra money for such luxuries. Patterns for a young girl's clothing were cut down from the gown the frontier woman was wearing—ruffles, ribbons and frills were not generally used for daily dress.

Children must do chores, and restrictive clothing was not at all practical. Girls' dress was usually a dark color that hid the dirt, and would usually be covered by an easily laundered over-dress (apron or pinafore). The over-dress could be switched for another one while mother laundered the first. Buttons were priceless on the frontier, so most dresses were tied with an attached sash, which kept the whole outfit modestly together. Winter woolen dresses might be lined with last summer's calico to cut down on the itching. A lucky girl might have a Sunday dress, with perhaps a trimming of ribbon or lace. Undergarments were simple white cotton panels, which evolved into the lace-trimmed pantaloons as the 1800s evolved (with easily-removed leggings to assist with laundering), but the wool or cotton long stocking was the primary stock of school girls, topped by ankle-high button up leather boots, which were eminently practical in all weathers, and locations. Town girls had more of a heel on their boots, which tended to mud up on the frontier. Country girls often adopted the very useful Indian- style leather moccasin, which peeled off easily to keep the inside of the ox-wagon clean on long marches, where the wagon served as bedroom at nightfall and had to be kept as clean as possible. By the 1860s, families often had access to personal sewing machines, which dramatically helped mothers to follow patterns that the magazines published.

"For one dollar per year, the Butterick Publishing Company brought women across the country the latest styles and homemaking news. Women could purchase paper patterns for twenty-five to thirty cents and recreate in California the clothes of the Parisian; from 1873, *The Delineator* was one of the major fashion magazines." (www.loc.gov/exhibits/treasures).

Another source of fashion that women on the frontier might access was *Godey's Lady's Book*, which had the first female editor, Sarah Hale, who managed the magazine for forty years, from 1837 to 1877. This magazine had fashion plates, sentimental songs, recipes, and household hints (www.womenwriters.net/domestic goddess/ hale).

The layette (all things needed for the newborn) remained fairly constant—dressed in long gowns (for warmth?) "Napkins" or "nappies" in diaper weave linen (hence the name diapers) were secured with straight pins until the invention of the "safety" pin in 1849...new mothers were instructed to obtain multiples of every baby item as laundering was an arduous task. (Kent

State University Museum/ Centuries of Childhood Exhibition)

Skirts for girls were floor-length before the nineteenth century, but as the 1800s progressed, girls began to have the freedom of a shortened dress style, which was less expensive for Western mothers. At eighteen, the dress must be to the ground, but a sixteen-year-old wore skirts to the ankle, a fourteen-year-old's dresses were to the calf, and for girls twelve and under the hem was to just below the knee.

Outdoors, girls were expected to wear a hat. In the West these might be a simple hand-sewn bonnet, or a straw box-type of hat.

Coats were usually of the cape style, which could be serviceable for many years of growth and used as a seat out doors to keep a girl's dresses cleaner.

Synthetic dyes were becoming available in the 1860s, and so the traditional dark colors children wore gave way to intensely bright choices. Plum, puce, scarlet reds, and navy colors now brightened children's clothing.

Dough-Nuts

For dough-nuts, take one pint of flour, half a pint of sugar, three eggs, a piece of butter as big as a egg, and a teaspoon of dissolved pear lash. When you have no eggs, a gill of lively emptings will do; but in that case, they must be made overnight. Cinnamon, rose-water, or lemon-brandy, if you have it. If you use part lard instead of butter, add a little salt. Do not put in until the fat is very hot. The more fat they are fried in, the less they will soak fat.

Lydia Maria Child, "The American Frugal Housewife".
Twelfth Edition. Boston: Carter, Hendee, and Co. 1833
www.food books.com/recipes.htm.

volunteer their side room for the lessons, and this same family had an older sister of almost eighteen who could read and do figures and was game to try out being the teacher, thinking to earn a bit of spending money from the children's folks.

It was not more than a week after we had settled in when the ladies of the camp called a meeting to discuss the new school. Invitations were sent out to all the nearby ranches with school-age children, and anticipation was high among all the families.

Mother was one of the most interested, and was happy to offer the lodging house main room for the ladies to gather in. Times were tight, but this was a big occasion, so Mother had me and my newfound girl friends lined up to serve coffee and fresh doughnuts.

Of course all the children heard about doughnuts being served and you could smell them all over the settlement, so mother made a point to make plenty. Mother always said the bit of flour was worth the goodwill.

Well, the school meeting was opened by several of the previous settlers, and it sure seemed like a lot of time was spent discussing the when, the where, the costs, the times, the why, and all sorts of points not of interest to a giggling passel of five-to-nine- year-olds—it seems that the girls of ten and eleven could sit quiet—but the rest of us took off playing school and practicing for recess, and strictly avoiding any contact with the boys.

Mother had let me try out my second- best dress with my new boots, so you can believe I did spend some of the time worrying about the dust getting on them. But suddenly I got tagged "it," and I guess that was when my boots got their first breaking- in. Mother looked so very pleased over the compliments to her baked goods and the fact that school was really going to commence the following week, that perhaps she did not notice my scuffs—but she sure had my moccasins set out for me to put on while I did a bit of polishing on the boots as quick as the meeting broke up. Just like with everything, Mother always was a step ahead of me.

Later that evening, after all the boarders were fed and accounted for, mother brought out the small package left by my uncle. I was so very excited, thinking how great things were with new shoes and playmates and now a surprise!

Mother let me carefully open the brown paper (she set it aside to use for something later) and you could have knocked me over with a feather—inside were real, honest schoolbooks!

The first was truly a gift from Uncle Will. After the brothers had walked all the way to California in 1860, the War between the States commenced. Uncle Will was American through to the bone and he walked back home, enlisted in the Union side, and signed up with the Third Regimental Wisconsin Cavalry, with his younger brother Elijah joining a different company. After the fighting was over he came back to his Bodie, and the book he bought for me was Will all over. In marvelous red, white, and blue, it was titled *THE UNION A B C*, and was an alphabet book with feelings just like Will's.

The Union A B C

A is America, land of the free
B is a Battle, our soldiers did see
C is a Captain, who led on his men
D is a Drummer Boy, called little Ben.
E is the Eagle, that proudly did soar.
F is our Flag, that shall wave evermore.
G is a Gun, that is used in the war.
H is for Hard-tack, you scarcely can gnaw.
I is for Infantry, who boldly advance.
J is for Jig, which the Contrabands dance.
K is for Knapsack, they carry along.

Degan, Estes & Company
No. 23 Cornhill, Boston

A Point Of Fact

W.A. Chalfant, the leading historian of the Owens Valley, in *The Story of Inyo* details Inyo County in 1869 as having three school districts—North of Fort Independence (Bishop Creek), Fort Independence, and South of the Fort. "Nothing has been unearthed from county records to show who first served as teachers of the children of the Inyo school districts. Fort Independence had a school house, and presumably a teacher.

The first school in northern Owens Valley, then belonging to Mono County, was supported by subscription, in 1866. In the early months of that year, with but one white child of school age in the territory, no school was established." On the arrival of Mr. and Mrs. Joel Smith and six children in March, and with many other families settling, Mrs. Smith began her school. Later on, the first public school teacher north of Independence was Milton S. Clark, at Bishop.

On January 1, 1869, the Rev. Andrew Clark established the Baptist Church at Bishop Creek, the first religious establishment in eastern California, and began holding services for the surrounding 100 miles, on horseback.

During the season of 1869 the valley's estimated grain production was 250 tons: lands cultivated amounted to 5,000 acres. Home mills were producing flour and lumber for all needs.

Well, yes, to me it was just the most beautiful book any child could or should ever have.

Mother wasn't as thrilled, on account it having lots to do with the War, and I guess most women didn't think that the War Between the States was so grand as the menfolk did. Mother didn't want to bring up a sore subject with our Southern-sympathizing neighbors in Bishop—but she told me it was a fine gift, and I should straightaway write and thank Uncle Will. Perhaps we would keep it special at home for the two of us to share, and not risk it getting torn at school. Mother always had the good ideas, didn't she?

The other book Mother was very pleased with, as it was called:

THE ECLECTIC FIRST READER FOR YOUNG
CHILDREN
WITH PICTURES
BY W.H. McGUFFEY
PROFESSOR AT MIAMI UNIVERSITY, OXFORD

And that was just on the cover. Inside, there were just pages of words and lessons and I am afraid I did think otherwise of this schooling mother was so keen about. To be sure, there were lots of drawings of proper children behaving themselves with the best of manners. It did not seem any of these children had ever been to the West or had ever heard of Bodie, let alone the Bishop Creek School, held in a side room taught by the oldest sister of our neighbor.

The Story Of The Mcguffey Readers

It is reported in the online encyclopedia (wickipedia.com) that early American schools' used two basic teaching manuals. These were the New England Primer of the eighteenth century and the McGuffey's Eclectic Readers of the nineteenth century. The latter book sold at least 120 million copies as of 1960, ranking it with the Bible and Webster's Dictionary.

William Holmes McGuffey was born September 23, 1800 in Pennsylvania. McGuffey had been a teacher in many one-room school houses across frontier Ohio and Kentucky. Self-educated and valuing his own family's Scottish religious beliefs, William McGuffey believed that "religion and education needed to be interrelated and was essential to a healthy society" (Wikipedia.com). McGuffey taught language at Miami University in Oxford, Ohio. He married Harriet Spinning and was father to five children.

America's schools were outgrowing the New England Primer. The publishing company of Truman and Smith took the recommendation of Harriet Beecher Stowe, asking McGuffey to create a series of reading books for elementary school students.

The original readers were completed in the 1830s and contained stories, poems, essays, and speeches reflecting the authors' moral beliefs as well as experiences gained teaching in frontier classrooms. The readers were "filled with stories of strength, character, goodness, and truth." (Wikipedia.com)

Also key to modern education philosophies, the *McGuffey Readers* were the first textbooks to promote the phonics method, which is based on an emphasis of letter and word recognition. Another element that was to epitomize modern education is that the readers progressed from the very basic to advanced levels, gradually introducing a new and more sophisticated vocabulary. The readers used real works of great literature.

Historical Perspective

Russell Freedman presents the history of schooling in the pioneer West in *Children of the Wild West*. Using firsthand memories of the descendants of the settlers, Freedman corroborates that as settlers first moved into western areas, there were "no schools of any kind." Children were home schooled by their parents or by neighbors, and because most parents were extremely busy just carving out a home and a livelihood, often there was no adult to teach the basics and no materials to use. Many pioneers had just completed the overwhelming journey of their lives from the East, and items such as arithmetic or reading primers were either not brought along or were discarded with other precious household items.

But education has always been a great cultural value in the United States, and families yearned for organized schools for their youngsters. As soon as the basic necessities were achieved, families would "band together to put up a proper school."

"The first schoolhouse was usually a simple cabin built of logs, sod, or adobe...with dirt floors...no running water..."and dogs came to school with their young masters. There were "no blackboards, no charts, maps... and textbooks were scarce"

"Classroom time was devoted to the three R's, along with American history and geography. Students memorized grammar rules, recited history, practiced penmanship, read aloud, and competed in spelling bees."

Pupils were not separated into grades; the teacher could work with one or two students at the same level while the others studied quietly. Older students frequently tutored younger students.

Teachers were especially hard to procure in the California mining camps, and some teachers were barely older than their pupils. Pay was very low, and might be little above room and board, between ten and thirty-five dollars for the three-to-four-month school term.

California did not make education compulsory until 1874, when a new law required all children between eight and fourteen years to attend class for at least two-thirds of the school year.

Bodie (Photo by Author)

CHAPTER THREE:

CALICO AND SILK

"Imagination can picture these streets, now silent as death, once teaming with the affairs of men; stages from one place or another rolling in, bringing the calico of virtue and the silk of vice…"

–William Arthur Chalfant, 1868-1943
Gold, Guns & Ghost Towns

My mother held her head high. Deserted for the lust of gold, as so many wives were in those years, it was her decision to make a stand for me, her daughter.

My father had given her a choice; move on to new untamed places where he believed unknown fortunes could be made—or stay here in this high valley of the Sierras, where naysayers believed that the best was past.

As a child, I cried for my absent father. As an adult, I admired my mother—She never seemed to falter. She was up at the break of light, preparing breakfast for travelers, cattlemen and wanderers; all with that calm smile and quiet greeting. Pressing the beds back together for the next paying customer, mopping, dusting the dirt that seemed to seep in from everywhere, sweeping again, cooking over a stove that seemed cooler than the summer sun outside the door, all with, if not a smile, a pleasantness and a hospitable nature that endeared her to and earned her the respect of all whom chance brought her way.

Eighteen-seventy came and went. My mother worked six-and-a-half days a week, putting by pennies, a dollar or two, and sometimes more. Her brothers also struggled financially, hunting for the big break. Rodger Horner and Aunt Marietta delayed their own departure for Wisconsin, because with my uncles Ben and Wilson, it seemed like the rich discovery of a lifetime was just around that next blasting. Drifts were dug and burrowed this way and that, searching for the precious metal that would put the whole miserable business into a golden light. Always, hope glowed brighter than fact.

My mother seemed glad to be rid of the constant expectation and disappointment of the Bodie goldfields. Among the ranchers' wives and farming folk, Mother found gentleness and a respect for hard work, and the kindness that she missed in the company of the miners, who were always focused on their dangerous underground mission.

Through 1871 and '72, Mother grew to miss her brothers terribly. News of them, their families, and their day-to-day ups and downs were her hidden treasure.

If the post did not bring news, travelers brought letters and presents—specially sent to Mother and me to keep the circle of family tight around us.

One particular gentleman, who was associated with Ben and Wilson, came very regularly to our community for his cattle and dairy business. Mr. Almond Huntoon seemed to be a frequent visitor to our lodging house. Mr. Huntoon was especially solicitous to Mother.

She, as a married lady, held a certain respect in her circle. As a married lady, receiving visits from a gentleman other than family created a precarious social situation. It is true Father was long gone, and with little news from him it seemed that we were lost forever between what was desirable—a family—and what was respectable. Mr. Huntoon's visits became more frequent and lasted longer, and I was aware that mother would have to make a choice soon, or lose her status among the good women of the town.

Fate stepped in. An urgent letter came by post. Ben's wife Mary was gravely ill and the care of my two small cousins Will and Harry was sending Aunt Mary into exhaustion. Would my mother please come at once? Her brother was at his wit's end with dread and worry.

Helen Anne Kernohan in the Late 1870s
Mono County Historical Society Photo

Mother decided we must return to Bodie. Mr. Huntoon was very helpful. He sent not himself, which might have shaded mother's departure, but a ranch hand to fetch us. If Ben's abode was not enough room for us, Mr. Huntoon had a farmhouse in the Booker Flats area of Cottonwood Canyon which, by chance, was much closer than Bishop Creek for helping Ben and his family.

Mr. Huntoon and his brother Moses were landowners and pioneers in the Big Meadows area. Moses bought 320 acres of this land from the General Land Office between 1874 and '75. Hard work rewarded the brothers, and with mining experiencing a revival in the Bodie camp, they thought to start up a lodging house to cash in on some of this new excitement.

The brothers approached Mother with their idea and Mother, I think, surprised both men with her answer: "I wish to be a full partner. I have my own nest egg to invest and if you wish to take on a partner, I am for you."

The idea of a woman as a partner in a going business was something as new as this gold country. Women were wives or flirtations. They stayed in the background and men made the decisions—when to stay, when to sell. But Mother had been through the despair of losing one husband. She would not place herself on the weak side of any business again.

I think the other brother bowed out politely, but Almond had developed a great respect for Mother. Her stubbornness and independence did not intimidate him. A calico-dressed, hard-working woman on the frontier was more valuable than gold, if a man could but see, and Almond Huntoon was a man who could see. Mother and Mr. Huntoon shook hands on the deal and became business partners.

There was a great change about to hit Bodie. The quiet backward camp was fading, and in its place was a whole new vision—a town was coming. Saws were cutting wood, hammers were pounding nails, and streets were laid out.

Gold, gold, we have gold. It was 1877 and the news had spread around the world. The Bodie miners hit the incredible Fortuna Ledge, and the gold vein was leading deep and true, creating one of the last of America's great nineteenth-century gold bonanzas.

Some men mined it; others lent capital and owned the gold. And many others were there to catch the gold as the miners and the capitalists flung it about. This time, for sure, Mother and Mr. Huntoon were going to catch the gold.

Mother had decided finally to return to our home! To Bodie! I was so excited, because for me Bodie had stayed in my dreams as the most solid place of my life—family was there. My two uncles had followed one hope after another and had begun to see small payoffs turn to moderate gains. Both had sidelined their golden quests. Wilson's blacksmithing business was growing and prospering, and Ben had his hand in several directions—land sales, wood contracting and various gold mines.

Mother returned to Bodie as a bona fide businesswoman—her relationship with father brought to a legal conclusion, she was now free in this new Bodie to make a commitment to Almond Huntoon. They were engaged to be married in the New Year—1878, that is. I myself was almost a grown woman—I would be celebrating my sixteenth birthday on my return to Bodie.

Our life was about to change. What a difference the last eight years had worked on little Bodie! Was it a mining camp or a full-blown town? From the scattered, humble mining cabins with no stores, no stages, nothing, to—my good heavens—real civilization!

Mother threw herself into her new business venture—along with checking on Aunt Mary Butler, making meals for us all, laundry, cleaning, mending—you best believe she kept me busy as well, running errands for both family and our new hotel, the Booker Flat.

I loved to walk the new boards outside of stores filled to the brim with anything our family might need, and many things we didn't need.

Gillson & Barber

Would respectfully announce to the inhabitants of Bodie, and surrounding country, that they are receiving and opening out a large and well selected stock for general merchandise, consisting in part of

GROCERIES,

PROVISIONS,

GRAIN, FLOUR,

GROUND FEED,

LIQUERS,

CLOTHING,

HATS, CAPS, BOOTS, SHOES

CROCKERY

TINWARE,

STOVES,

HARDWARE,

PAINTS, OILS,

PATENT MEDICINES

ETC. ETC. ETC.

We propose selling these goods:

Cheaper than heretofore sold in this section of the country.

From our long experience in business, eligible location, gentlemanly and obliging clerks, we feel confident that we can guarantee satisfaction to all who may favor us with their patronage.

Call and examine before purchasing elsewhere.

Nov 7, 1877

The Bodie Standard

PALACE
Shaving ad Hair Dressing Saloon,
Opposite Gilson & Barber's New Store,
BODIE,……………………………CALIFORNIA

Hair cutting a specialty.
Prof. W.N. NERBETT……………Proprietor
11-7-1877
The Bodie Standard

BUSINESS,
Mining & Law Office
Of
C. ESTABROOK SMITH
Main Street………………Bodie
(Opposite the old spring)
All Business entrusted to Him
Will receive careful attention and will be
Done in accordance with the law.
11-7-77
The Bodie Standard

Wm. H. Dolman,
Dealers In
FEED, LUMBER, AND WOOD.
Corner Main and Green Sts.
BODIE…………………………California

C. W. MILLS,
Carpenter and Builder
Shop-South Main Street

BODIE..................California
General jobbing promptly attended to.
Furniture carefully repaired.
Nov. 7, 1877, The Bodie Standard

GOLD

But a few short months ago Bodie was an insignificant little place, now she is rapidly growing in size and importance and people are crowding in upon her from far and near, and why? Because of the rich discoveries of gold, yellow, glittering precious gold, the base of man and yet his antidote, his blessing and his curse, his happiness and misery... the rich man's strength and the poor man's weakness.

Nov. 7, 1877, The Bodie Standard

Poor Mail Facilities in Bodie

Will you please inform your readers why the present mail facilities between this camp and the outside world are in such a demoralized condition? ...This camp is growing in importance every day, and judging from present appearances we will have a large emigration here in the spring , and I do think we are, and will be of sufficient importance for the postal agent of the coast to pay us some attention, and remedy these existing evils.

Nov. 7, 1877, The Bodie Standard

Mrs. Murray and Mrs. McDonald have opened a restaurant one door north of Strowbridge's saloon, South Main Street.

Nov. 7, 1877, The Bodie Standard

Improvements.—Building in Bodie for the week past has been going on as rapidly as any time this fall. Everyone seems very anxious to get their lumber as fast as possible from Bridge-port…a great many residences have been built. We are glad to hear the click of the hammer, and the buzzing saw in Bodie from morning until night.

Nov. 7, 1877, The Bodie Standard

A Great many strangers come to Bodie daily, to take a look at our mines. They seem to go away well satisfied that they have seen the gold king of the world.

Nov. 7, 1877, The Bodie Standard

A GOOD MOVE.—Our citizens are about to organize a fire department for the protection of their property. We hope to see all of our business men lend a helping hand to assist the boys along, for this is something much needed.

Nov. 7, 1877, The Bodie Standard

Our merchants for the past week have received about sixty tons of merchandise. Gilson & Barber received out of this about forty-two tons.

Nov. 7, 1877 The Bodie Standard

Post Office
NEWS DEPOT AND BOOK STORE
Bodie, Cal. Aurora, Nev.
A full supply of the latest
ATLANTIC, PACIFIC, AND EUROPEAN
Newspapers & Periodicals.
BLANK BOOKS
FINE STATIONARY,
PENS AND INK

BLANK CARDS,
And every variety of articles normally found in
School and stationary store.
Give us a call,
SILAS B. SMITH
Nov. 7, 1877, The Bodie Standard

The weather for the past week has been delightful. Last Tues-
day night we had a light fall of snow, which barely covered the
ground, but on Wednesday morning when the sun made its
appearance the snow had vanished.
Nov. 7, 1877, The Bodie Standard

The ball at Brown's new hotel, on the evening of November
12th, promises to be a very successful affair. The gents are look-
ing over their wardrobe and the ladies are getting their fixings
in order. A pleasant and enjoyable time will, no doubt, be had.
Nov. 7, 1877, The Bodie Standard

PAY-DAY—Last Monday the Standard company paid out
$40,000 o its employees, wood contractors and our merchants.
Nov. 7, 1877, The Bodie Standard

Bodie is as lively as ever; new arrivals every day; Virginia
City, Gold Hill, San Francisco and other portions of the coast
contributing daily of their best and most energetic citizens to make
up a thriving city in the near future, here upon this flat, where
but a year ago, a score of miners were picking away for a bare
subsistence. Wonders will never cease in this great country of ours.
Nov. 7, 1877, The Bodie Standard

WILSON BUTLER,
Blacksmith and Wagon Maker,
Aurora, Nev.   *Bodie, Cal.*
Particular attention paid to
HORSE AND OX SHOEING
By the best workmen at reasonable rates
All Kinds Of
WAGON MATERIAL, IRON, ETC,
For Sale
Wagons Made Or Repaired
Agent for the favorite
NEVADA STANDARD WAGONS
Delivered at Carson prices to purchasers to
Aurora, Bodie, Bridgeport, or Sweetwater.
Wilson Butler
Nov. 7, 1877, The Bodie Standard

BODIE & AURORA
STAGE LINE.
Franklin & Thompson… Proprietors
Leaves Aurora for Bodie daily on the
arrival of stages from Carson.
Leaves Bodie for Aurora daily at
3 o'clock P.M.
Making close connection
With stages for
Carson, Bellville, and Benton
FARE…………………………$2.00
C. Novacovich, Agent, Aurora
W.A. Atlee, Agent, Bodie
Nov. 7, 1877, The Bodie Standard

You might think Mother would be too busy to mind my school-ing, but you did not know her. My cousins Will and Harvey were of school age as well, and Mother set about with the other ladies of the camp to find the solution for this.

Women were not following behind the men on the issue of schools. Many a busy husband would arrive home from the shop, the mines, the banks, or the farm to face his wife standing in the kitchen—dinner not served up—listening to the mothers of school-age children demand that a teacher be found and hired and that a suitable building be located, purchased, or built.

Creative offers poured in. Living rooms were offered as tempo-rary schoolrooms. The members of the newly-built Miners Union Hall thought that the space could be lent to Bodie's scholars. Unrented office spaces, a rare commodity, were also considered.

At first, the school was at an available house with an extra room (in the daytime, at least, since rarely was a room empty at night). There were eight to a dozen scholars anxious to learn their letters. The first real teacher I recall was Miss Belle Donnally.

But families kept a-moving into our Bodie, and those that lived there already had more and more children that needed schooling, so the school was moved to the side room of the Cary building on South Main Street. Reports say that the school increased rapidly from the original 10 pupils to 40 in the first two weeks, and had increased to almost 76, ages 5 to 17 were enrolled in the school by the end of the first three month session. The children overflowed the Cary building just as the town hurried to build its first real school building up on Green Street across the creek. But this first school was not long with us and was destroyed by a sudden fire. Rumors that this first school on Green Street was brought down by one of the older boys with a set of matches (who preferred hang-ing about Main Street to learning his lessons) became one of the most popular tidbits of the summer picnic discussions. This mystery went the way of old Bill Bodey's gold mine, gradually fading out of the news.

The town purchased the Bon Ton Lodging House, and this two-story building was moved to the Green Street site at the side of Bodie Creek. That is the building where I spent the best years of my childhood, playing with friends in the schoolyard, sharing lunches and sweating in the heat of the potbelly stove that kept us warm in summer and winter alike.

It took some time to get all the families organized, but enthusiasm was very high and finally, by January, a beginning was settled on.

> *Public School—On Monday the first term of the first public school in Bodie commenced. The school for present is located at the residence of Mrs. J. W. Dawley and is under her management.*
>
> *–Jan. 9, 1878, The Bodie Standard*

> ## Notice
>
> *Notice is hereby given to the public that the citizens of Bodie have petitioned for a division of Bridgeport School District for the purpose of forming a new school district, called the Bodie School District.*
>
> *A.M. HAYS*
> *Co. Sup't of Mono Co.*
> *Bridgeport, Oct 26, 1877*

The Board of Supervisors met at the court house in Bridge-port on Monday, Nov. 5th...Quite a number of bills were allowed. The Bodie school district was paid out...

—Nov. 1877, The Bodie Standard

Public School- Our public school was opened on last Tuesday morning, Mrs. Belle Donald (Donnelly), teacher with ten scholars. Mrs. Donnally is a graduate of the State Normal School Of Massachusetts, and is very highly spoken of as a teacher. We are glad to see our citizens so much interested in the welfare of their children in getting a school started here, for it is one of the first institutions needed in a mining camp.

—The Bodie Standard

Mar. 18, 1878

School.—Our reporter visited the Public School yesterday and was much surprised to see such a large attendance, there now being twenty-five children in regular attendance. Miss Belle Donnally, the teacher, informed him that there are yet some children in the district who are not attending school.

—The Bodie Standard

April 3, 1878

Petition of the citizens of Bodie for School District granted and boundaries of said district to be the same as those of the Bodie road district.

—The Bodie Standard

May 15, 1878

Alex Nixon, President (Bodie Miners' Union), has offered the Miners' Union Hall in this place to the School Trustees, free of charge.

–The Bodie Standard
May 22, 1878

THE SCHOOL—The School Trustees being unable to secure a house, school was not opened last Tuesday. It is thought a building can be secured by next Monday, at which time school will commence.

–The Bodie Standard
May 27, 1878

*Monday was rather a windy day
School opened Monday with 20 scholars.*

–The Bodie Standard
May 1878

School Matters.—Many of our readers are perhaps unaware that an election was held on the 10th of August upon the question of raising a tax for the purpose of building a school-house in Bodie, and that it was decided to levy a tax of $2,500 to be devoted to that purpose. The Board of School Directors, Col. S.B. Furguson, Dr. J. L. Berry and Dr. D. V. Goodson, selected Captain G. L. Porter as assessor and collector of the tax, and Captain Porter has appointed L.N. Snyder as his deputy. Mr. Synder is now engaged in making the assessment. The large influx of families in Bodie at present renders more extensive school facilities absolutely necessary, and for $2,500 the amount voted, we should have a very good building.

–The Bodie Standard
Aug. 1878

Bodie School
Green Street, Bodie

Sketch by Author

Teachers on the Frontier

As the United States expanded westward to California, the frontier schools moved as well. Public education was not ordained in our constitution, and wealthy families could afford private teachers. Poor families did the best they could. It was about 1830 or so that reformers took up the cry for publicly-funded and universal (read: white) access. It was as much to teach common American (Christian) values as it was to educate that education of all children became to be a political reality passed by each State. Massachusetts became the first to pass compulsory, free, public education in 1852, and by 1883 most of the western states had followed its lead. All states had laws for children to attend elementary school by 1918.

Teachers in the first frontiers of Ohio and Kentucky were generally men, and many were not qualified to teach more that the basics of reading, writing, and arithmetic. As the nineteenth century progressed, quality education, with required subjects and trained teachers, became the norm in the eastern states. The frontiers had the desire for education but little funding, and teacher salaries were so low that most of the men could make more at farming or mining. The public school, or common school as it was usually called, was funded by local property taxes and charged no tuition, but was only open to white children. Schools were later created for non-white children, but these were usually segregated. Some were boarding situations where the children might be involuntarily separated from their mothers and fathers for many years. These were often funded as missionary ventures, and the strict Christian philosophy of the teachers was a very cold change for the children, already terrified by separation from their families.

As men moved into ventures more profitable than teaching in mid-century, many women's advocates, such as Catherine Beecher, started to promote female teachers to fill this void. But the high tone of the speeches in the East did little to prepare these single women for their professional duties and the culture shock of moving away from the security of eastern institutions. Often the new teacher found herself bunking with her pupils in complete isolation from the comforts of towns. The classrooms were sparsely furnished, and schoolbooks might be nonexistent, or at best outdated and worn. In the typical one-room school, children of all ages and abilities would be grouped together, and often discipline was difficult.

Women were willing to work for lower wages than men, because for them, the West was becoming the land of opportunity. In the East, the protective but rigid society held little for females outside of marriage-women were not allowed to work, were usually not the title holder on their own lands, and were often left to a life of spinsterhood if marriage did not occur at an age suitable for childbearing. In the West, women had a better chance to find a husband, to own their own land, and to break out of an unhappy life dictated by strict moral codesthat relaxed the farther women got from the big Eastern town. Only single women were allowed to teach, and as the teachers found husbands they had to give up their jobs. By one estimate, by 1870 over 25 percent of all American-born white women had taught at some point in their lives.

Schoolhouses, as public buildings, were often used for the center of more than just teaching the children. Often the empty classroom could be used for itinerant ministers in need of a place to hold indoor services.

School programs, where the children demonstrated their singing and poem reciting, were a regular part of the frontier social calendar, during which food was often shared and perhaps some community singing occurred.

As the frontier towns became more settled, standards of curriculum and teacher training became part of the progress of the West's growing civilization. Every locality with six or more children qualified to have a teacher. Western towns paid teachers higher salaries and credentials became more important.

Bodie Historical Museum (Photo by Author)

CHAPTER FOUR:
TEMPLES, DREAMS, AND ASHES

Of the 11,794 Chinese living in California (in 1852), only seven were women. By 1870, 3,536 Chinese women had immigrated to California, 61 percent (2,157) listed as prostitutes.

–The Chinese in California 1850-1925
Memory.loc.gov/collections/Chinese/history

The 1880 United States Federal Census records approximately 357 persons of the Chinese race, twenty-two of whom were female, living in the township of Bodie, Mono County, California. Of the women recorded, thirteen were listed as married, and nine were listed as single—all were listed as ranging in age from nineteen to thirty-two. No Chinese children were listed.

My name is Pearl Zheng. My grandfather, Lao Ma, was blessed with six sons, and very late in his life with one very puny girl child, my mother. While she had a beautiful name, mostly she was called Xiao Chi Tzu, which in your language means "Little Seventh Child." It probably seems funny to you to call a child by a number, but her birth at grandfather's age of fifty-eight was a sign of his great virility, and he was honored for his seventh daughter.

Six big, strong sons gave grandfather his dignity. His family name is Ma, with the honorific addition of "Lao," which some translate into English as "old one," but which in our culture is a term of respect, designating that that person is a wise man.

I was born high in the Sierra Nevada Mountains in 1870. In Chinese, you would call me Zheng Chu-Li, because our people place our family name first—just like in real life. The Chinese place family first.

Our home in Bodie was not as illustrious as grandfather would wish, but we were still a strong family of six sons with humble obedient wives, and many offspring to carry on grandfather's place in the afterworld with honor.

When I was a small child, I loved to sit at grandfather's side and ask him to tell me stories of the old days in Shandong Province, of how our family came to Gold Mountain (California), of when I was born, and of how the Ma family came to live in Bodie. This is the story Grandfather told me, as he patiently sipped tea from a tiny cup.

We, the Ma family, go back many, many generations in the celebrated middle kingdom. Our place in Lao-Shan was for many hundred years blessed with healthy sons and beautiful women. In saying so, Grandfather would slightly wink at me to compliment me. Many of the great thinkers of the middle kingdom Zhong Gua, or China, lived and breathed the same pure air as our family.

But drought came to our countryside, and for ten years we were struggling to scratch out the millet from the fields. Even the apple trees began to dry up.

When a man came and told of the riches to be had in the Gold Mountain, California, over the ocean, and about the need for a great many skilled men to build the railroad to connect the Gold Mountain with the eastern oceans of America—Grandfather bravely stepped forward for our village.

Grandfather went to the temple on Lao-Shan and cast the bamboo sticks and burned three sticks of incense. He recalled vividly the message that the fortune teller drew out of his request: "Flow with the small streams and lay low until reaching the great ocean." With these words from the sacred book of the Tao, Grandfather saw that he must now take a new path through life.

Grandfather went to the other men of his village, who were also in hard times and just about starving. He was able to look at the sad eyes of their families and say "The Ma family will go to America and build the railroad—who will come with us to grasp this golden chance?"

Grandfather's eyes were very black, and as he looked back to that day, I could detect just small tone of regret. Many of the villagers did decide to come with the Ma family—the bold and the strong were ready. Grandmother was very ill. She wished to stay at her family home and not look upon this strange new country, America. Grandmother wished her seventh daughter to stay, but my mother, Ma Xiao Chi, could not bear the separation from her beloved father and brothers.

There was great concern for Xiao Chi's virtue in such a strange land, where the Chinese were not all from our village, honoring the Ma family. They decided to make over Xiao Chi from seventh daughter to seventh "son."

It was not so bad for her, grandfather explained. Chinese women modestly dressed in loose pants and long cotton jackets anyway. If Grandfather signed up seven sons, the white devils were really very stupid and they would never look any closer. And so my mother-to-be came to America dressed as a boy! Grandfather was right—the American man from the railroad never even looked at my mother. He just gave grandfather the tickets to the boat, and that was it.

Grandfather can read and write Chinese like a scholar—he knows hundreds of Chinese characters by heart—so it is nothing for him to relate every detail of our family's travels to America: the long voyage, the smell of the ocean, the food they ate, the first time they all saw San Francisco.

The railroad men did not wish any of their precious labor to be lost to either the gambling dens or the goldfields, so the Ma family and the others from Lao-Shan were moved away from San Francisco quickly, straight to the end of the railroad line. Within days of their arrival in America, all the Chinese from our village were hard at work. The work started in the foothills, but soon the rails needed to go across the great snowy peaks of the Sierras into the Territory of Nevada.

Once the railroad men got the Chinese here, it seemed all their promises went up in smoke—if a man did not work he was not fed. If he was not fed in this cold, unforgiving land, he froze to death and his bones were tossed to the side, far as far could be from his peaceful and rightful place with his ancestors.

The Ma family learned very quickly. The first thing they learned was whom to trust and whom not to—the first white devil on the line they encountered asked them their name, and Grandfather answered for the whole family, as was custom: "Ma." The man called out to the other blue-eyes: "Ah." Instantly, our entire family got our name changed. Grandfather never blinked. Later, he told his sons, what does it matter what the monkey calls us? We do not listen to the monkeys screeching in the woods, and we shall not listen to these fellows, either.

My grandfather's eldest son is Ma Ching, and he is the biggest and strongest. My first uncle did not like how discourteous these white men were. But Grandfather told them all to just work and take the money and soon enough we would be on our way to the real gold mountain.

The work on the railroad was backbreaking, dangerous, and poorly-paid. But the Ma family stuck together. Mother was the designated cook in the camp and spared the real dangers of the daily work. Little by little, the brothers distinguished themselves by learning English and settling disputes among the other laborers and acting as a bank the men who were now lost in a foreign land and suffering greatly without the comforts of China. The lives of the brothers began to change, and they began their own song: do the work, take the pay, and don't give the barbarians an inch to grab at your soul.

So one day led to another, and finally the railroaders completed their great work of linking the East to the West. They did not need the Chinese laborers anymore. With a last doling out of the script, all were dismissed. Most of the Chinese meant to return home, but many decided to visit the gold camps on their way back, and perhaps make one last grasp for the riches they had envisioned when they were in their humble mud houses in the yellow lands.

Grandfather became very serious as he told me that the Chinese now mostly understood that they were not welcome in California. And in turn, Grandfather explained, the Chinese had no great fondness for the Americans they had met. The Chinese were laughed at because of their long queues and their traditional dress, robbed whenever possible, and shunned most of all. Grandfather was incensed at these facts. He knew that the Chinese are a people with two thousand years of culture, beliefs, science, and law, and with enough self-respect to block out most of the more hurtful and ignorant treatment.

Grandfather told me how the Chinese would bind together in their own cultural cocoons, within their own cultural walls. Chinatowns were created so they could live their lives, transplanting a tiny bit of the middle kingdom. Again, they felt at home speaking their own language, dressing in traditional clothes, and cooking their own food instead of foreign meals.

Left in the middle of nowhere like the other Chinese railroad workers, Grandfather and the Ma brothers now decided to go back to California, where using their new skills they would make a try at success in this new land. Grandfather said they had all given up on returning to their dried-up village. Word had come of Grandmother having joined her ancestors several months ago, so even Grandfather had no great wish to return to his homeland until after his body had turned to ashes.

The family agreed to head for the Genoa-Carson area in Nevada Territory. Ma Ching owned a wagon now, and his own team. He could make a living driving supplies for other Chinese.

The second Ma son had met a good businessman on the track work—Zheng Hong. They decided to pursue opening a grocery store in Carson. All the family could get involved—stocking, supplying, selling, and making honest money from their countrymen.

It was a great joy to the brothers when Grandfather and Zheng Hong went to a matchmaker in Carson and decided that my mother could now safely shed her "seventh brother" status and marry Mr. Zheng. Several of the brothers were also ready for marriage, and they obtained permission from grandfather to select wives. The future looked bright for both the Ma and Zheng families. It was traditional for several couples to share happiness on the same day. Plans were made, and a large multiple wedding solidified the families in dignified relationships.

Times were good and bad, Grandfather said with a sad smile. It seems that Carson was only a fitting place for my illustrious entry into this world—the family had a bad time with a local Chinese man whom Grandfather would only say was "selling worse dreams than the white devils." As I grew older, I came to realize that opium was an addiction that would turn many Chinese into living ghosts, and many Chinese gangsters would happily supply the opium for a price.

The Ma family now started to hear of a town high in the mountains where a new chance was possible—a place they called Bodie. Was it the illusive gold mountain, Jin Shan, of which our family so far had only dreamed?

Grandfather sent the two eldest of his sons to take a look at Bodie. The number two son could speak very good English now and called himself Sam, and first son Ma Ching was a burly fellow who commanded respect from all around. They were absent perhaps six weeks, and when they came back to grandfather they were very excited. You see, the brothers had bought property along a

place called King Street, enough for a store for Sam, and a larger
building they

> *A Supply Of Chinamen From the Comstock- it appears that we
> are to have a Chinatown as well as other evidence of Pacific Coast
> civilization as the following from the Virginia Enterprise denotes:
> The population in the Chinese quarter of this city is said to have
> diminished nearly one-half in the last year. Many of the residents of
> that section have taken their donkeys and "skipped out" for Bodie...*
>
> –The Bodie Standard
> *January 1878*

The Starving Chinese

*The telegraph still continues to bring reports from the north-
ern provinces of China that seventy millions of beings are on
the verge of starvation. This condition of affairs has been
caused by drought and failure of crops. In a country so densely
populated as these provinces, and where the people barely grow
enough to sustain life from one harvest to another, it is appall-
ing to think of the suffering caused by one short crop...*

*We cannot doubt that if the Chinese have found their way to
America from the comparatively prosperous eastern provinces in
thousands, that they will pour forth in myriads from the famine
stricken districts of the north as soon as a way is open to them.
The Chinese difficulty may speedily become a greater menace
to the United States...if the Chinese tide once begins to flow in
force, it is difficult to see where and when it will stop.*

–The Bodie Standard
March 1877

The Chinese of San Francisco have demanded protection against the fulfillment of threats made against them by the labor agitators headed by Kearney and Day. They intimated that they are prepared for an attack and will defend themselves to the bitter end.

–The Bodie Standard
October 1877

As odd as it is to Europeans and Westerners in general, there are a limited number of actual Chinese surnames. The Chinese language is composed of single syllable words, and most of the recorded 438 surnames are also one syllable. There are 10 major surnames: Zhang, Wang, Li, Zhao, Chen, Yang, Wu, Liu, Huang, Zhou. As the list continues there does not appear to be the surname "Ah" which is listed so predominately on the 1880 Bodie Census. The closest actual surname is "Ma" (by sound).

–The Origins of Chinese Surnames at Asiarecipe.com

The United States government took its first official stance on Chinese immigration in 1868 when, pressured by the railroad companies wanting cheap labor, it negotiated a policy of open immigration with China in the Burlingame Treaty. Chinese immigrants comprised 90 percent of the laborers who laid tracks eastward from Sacramento across the Sierra Nevada and Rocky Mountains to connect with the Union Pacific crews laying tracks across the Great Plains.

http://memory.loc.gov.learn.collections

sought to set up as a Chinese boardinghouse. Third brother Ma Kee would manage this venture. The other brothers, Sing and Wong, and baby brother Joe could help out running an eating room inside the lodging house to keep all the money under the family's control. The family was very hopeful that it finally would have its big break—until everyone looked at Grandfather's face.

When Grandfather told this part of the story, he always paused. Usually he said his tea was cold, could I please make more? Or he said he was weary of my silly questions and he was an old, tired man ready to join his ancestors.

Since I was sitting behind Ba-Ba's, my father's grocery store in the building next to Ma Kee's boarding house, I should have known the end of the story. But I always wanted to hear Grandfather tell it in his slow, patient voice, wandering among all the various details I was too small to remember clearly.

"My sons are no longer my sons," Grandfather said, not sadly but thoughtfully.

In Zhong-Gua, China, sons never tell their father what he, the head of the clan, will do, and where he will lay down his head. This only happens in this strangely beautiful land of the golden mountains. Sons forget the old ways and rush ahead of their elders into the very fire. "My wisdom is now useless, and I am treated like an old nanny, discarded to sit by the hearth, and once the children have grown, who knows what will become of me?"

Sons should ask their father for advice, he said, and the father goes to the temple and asks the divine ancestors, and all things will then fall into place, naturally.

"That has always been the way," Grandfather said. "Now the Way is ridiculed and men think that they have found a better, more modern way to live. But that it is my own sons! I pray for forgiveness."

Grandfather always ended the story there, no matter how much I pleaded and offered to make fresh, hot tea.

Mother always scurried me away at this point, comforting her father with a bit of fried pork, fixed in the traditional style with the vegetables Uncle Ching has fetched from our gardens. And Mother would now see it necessary to offer him a warm cup of plum wine, saved especially for the head of the Ma family.

In that new land, Bodie, with its beautiful lavender sunsets, my Grandfather preferred dreams of the old days on Lao-Shan. There at the Taoist temple, as a young man, he had placed the ashes of his own father, who had been revered and obeyed without question his entire life.

Now his sons struggled in this new land. The old ways were retreating and no one could turn back the hands of time. Rumors from China were of disruptions. Temples were being abandoned. In Chinese Taoist philosophy, it is inevitable that the decline would follow the fullness of the past.

Historical Points

Franklin Wedertz, in *Bodie: 1859-1900*, outlines a sympathetic chronicle of the Chinese living in Bodie from 1877 to 1883, the general time frame during which Bodie boasted a thriving Chinatown. Mr. Wedertz agrees that the early history of the Chinese in California was not one of the state's shining moments. The Chinese were ridiculed, feared, maligned, and physically abused. Economics played a part—if the job market had not been so tight, perhaps the better-natured citizens would have triumphed and welcomed these immigrants. As it was, the economy was tenuous and jobs were scarce, so the better citizens left them alone. This can be observed in the two leading newspapers of Bodie. The older, and perhaps therefore calmer, Folger Brothers of the *Daily Bodie Chronicle* were content to mention the Chinese only in regard to railroad labor facts, or in the judicial reports of court proceedings.

H. Z . Osborne of *The Daily Free Press* reflects the opposing point of view on the "Chinese Question," as well as many other political contests of the time. This paper takes an almost nasty delight in vilifying the Chinese residents of Bodie, almost daily publishing a negative, mocking account of various Chinese activities in Bodie. On at least two occasions, Anglo gentlemen were reported to have beaten Chinese launderers over lost shirts. The wording of the *Free Press* accounts stresses the righteousness of the attacks from the white man's perspective. As a historian, the necessity of the use of source materials is my only justification for quoting the *Free Press*—and often I have attempted to leave out the most salacious sentences.

According to Wedertz, the Chinese in most western camps would gather together. The Chinese in Bodie did so "for security and mutual protection." The Chinese did not blend into the American melting pot because of the hostility they encountered, and this caused the Chinese to depend on their own culture and language. "The common laborers were brought to California under contract to work for several years at low wages (from four to eight dollars a month). Often it was a Chinese capitalist who formed associations which gave out these contracts," Wedertz writes.

Much of Bodie's Chinese population had come from Virginia City early in 1878, and the 1880 census of Bodie places their number at approximately 357. "There were, however, many others at work in wood camps near Bodie," Wedertz writes. "Their small stone cabins are still visible in the canyons in and around Rough Creek and Clark Canyon, between Bodie and Bridgeport. This area was too rough for white labor to work profitably, yet the Chinese cut thousands of trees on the steep basaltic canyon walls. The wood was packed to King Street on mules. As the trees were cut, the smaller branches were burned to make charcoal. Many of these charcoal pits still dot the Bodie Hills, and it too was a rugged business. Only the frugal Chinese, and several Mexicans, were successful in the charcoal business. Charcoal had a variety of markets; the mills, blacksmiths and wash houses all used large amounts. The small buildings of the wash companies were crowded in among other buildings along King, Bonanza, and north Main Street. By the summer of 1882, many Chinese had left the camp to follow other mining excitements... By the end of 1882, King Street was about the most solemn and dreary spot in town."

Chinamen never write love letters to their sweethearts.
The Daily Free Press
Nov. 12, 1879
A Private Boarding House

*Gentlemen Wishing board by the Day or
Week can find everything to their satisfaction
On Wood Street
Opposite the Fashion Stables.
No Chinese Employed.
Cooking done by a genuine old Eastern
Lady cook.
Miss Tillie Barrows, Proprietress*
The Daily Free Press
May 11, 1880

A Jealous Chinaman
A Chinaman is liable to be as jealous as a white man and he gives vent to his pent up Utica just as ordinary people do when a rival is in the wood pile, so to speak. Yesterday afternoon (Mr.) Hop, a young china man, found a (person) of the Flowery Kingdom, casting almond eyes on a maiden fair of raven hair on King Street . Circus performance was instituted in which the outraged lover came out best...

–The Daily Free Press
June 3, 1880

China men with pack trains are doing a big business in the wood hauling line.

–The Daily Free Press
June 5, 1880

Hard to Digest

Yesterday forenoon a Chinaman Butchered a hog on King street...in the stomach was found a piece of silver watch chain about 3 inches long...the discovery created much merriment among the Celestial spectators...

–The Daily Free Press
June 5, 1880

The Carson and Colorado Railroad Fairly Begun.

The force of white laborers employed up to date of this issue number nearly three hundred men. Hey receive the equivalent of $2 per day, being comfortably lodged, well fed and paid $1 net per day.

The company have recently put on a gang of 100 Chinamen at Walker Lake, in a barren section where from lack of wood and water, white men have refused to work.

–The Daily Free Press
June 6, 1880

As a Chinese girl growing up in Bodie, my life was completely separate from view of the white children in town. The Bodie School did not open its doors to me. My grandfather would never have let me go there anyway. The knowledge of the white world had no value to Grandfather, and in this, Grandfather had the final say.

Grandfather was my teacher, and I learned to write in order to read the sacred books back to Grandfather in case his eyesight failed, and to do mathematics in order to make change to other Chinese residents who came into our establishment and purchased goods.

No white women ever came into our places of business. The white men who did were men who had business that was never any of mine, as I was scurried out of sight at the hint of their presence.

After the gold mines started to close in the early '80s, things got better for the few residents who decided to stay on King Street. Our laundering services were in high demand. Many of the finer families employed our men as cooks, and some of the women were hired to do light housekeeping chores, things that no white person could be found to perform. Now that my family had made the choice to stay in America, we began to look around us and saw the desperate lives that many of our countrymen endured.

As Chinese women, my mother, my aunts, and I became a rare treasure to the Ma family. Our men had wives, and could enjoy the blessing of children. But Chinese women of marriageable status were extremely rare and became almost nonexistent as new laws barred new arrivals from China.

Often women were bought as brides in the Chinese countryside, only to arrive as slaves in a trade that never allowed escape. Our family spoke in hushed voices of these tales of horror and dishonor in which terrible Chinese businessmen were the main profiteers.

I vowed to myself that when I grew up and married, my children would go to the western school and would learn all the ways of this new land, and therefore never become slaves to be lost forever. Of course I never told this dream to Grandfather. He was slipping more and more often, at least in his dreams, to find himself safely back in his homeland.

The 1880 United States Federal Census records the following persons living in Bodie of Chinese origin.

Ah Ching *thirty-eight years, married to a Chinese wife (twenty-six years), Occupation-Teamster.*

*Ah **Kee** thirty-seven years, married to a Chinese wife (twenty-four years), Occupation- owner of a Chinese lodging house.*

*Ah **Sing** thirty-two years, single, Occupation-cook at Jail*

*Ah **Sam** thirty years, married to a Chinese wife (twenty-nine years), Occupation-grocery store*

*Hing **Hong** twenty-nine years, married to a Chinese wife, Occupation-grocery store*

*Ah **Wong** twenty-nine years, married to a Chinese wife, Occupation- cook*

In Chinatown

Some Chinese have an eye for the beautiful. They are very few of course, but there are some. It is undoubtedly an acquired taste, and not inherited, if one may judge from the generality of Chinamen in Bodie. The Chinese quarters here are not extensive, but there are several neat and substantial structures, a good deal of money in circulation, and a quite extensive business carried on outside of the opium trade. One of the biggest establishments of the place was run by Tuong Yochg. A well selected supply of merchandize is in the store. The place is scrumptiously clean, and elaborately decorated.

–The Daily Free Press, *November*

Chinese American Relations

As the economy of California worsened in the late 1870s, political xenophobes pointed to the non-white residents, who had to work for bottom wages just to exist, as a scapegoat for white citizens losing their jobs.

The Chinese, with their cultural dress, language, and easily-discernible physical differences, became the whipping child of the tabloid press of the day. Citizens who might otherwise be more forgiving were exposed to a campaign of fear that the Chinese would soon outnumber the whites, and even take over control of the entire state.

Other races were tormented—Mexicans, native peoples, Italians—but the most serious prejudice seemed made to order for the Chinese people.

There were riots in San Francisco. A charismatic leader, Dennis Kearney, stepped in with his Workingmen's Party to challenge persons of Chinese descent to enjoy the equal rights of other Americans. The Workingmen's Party had political aspirations on a state and national level, and was even linked at one point with the expanding unionization of the workforce, including the Miners Union of Bodie.

Persons down on their luck, and perhaps inebriated, could find many other like- minded souls to commiserate with—the Chinese made perfect targets to vilify.

The culture of the Chinese, with two thousand years of philosophy, law, written language, poetry, and art did not give these new Asian-Americans a belief in their inferiority. The Chinese traditionally felt that the Europeans and Americans were the barbarians—and perhaps it was this justifiable pride that widened the gulf between the cultures and created resentment on both sides.

"By 1879, Congress passed a bill abrogating the section of the Burlingame Treaty that permitted unrestricted Chinese immigration, but President Hayes vetoed it. In 1882, with President Chester Arthur in office, Congress passed the Chinese Exclusion Act, prohibiting the immigration of Chinese laborers for ten years."

–The Library of Congress
The Learning Page/
The Chinese in California 1850-1925

Bodie Historical Museum
(Photo by Author)

CHAPTER FIVE:

ALL ABOARD FOR BODIE

My name is Alice E. Beck, and, I was born in California in the great year 1879. My daddy always said it that way: "The great year 1879," and I would ask him "What was so great about 1879?" Daddy would laugh and say with a lilt: "Why, my darling that was the year Your Sweetness was born and my life forever alighted!"

My daddy, Joseph E. Beck, lately of green Ireland, was very proud to be one of the swarm of men who worked with the sweat streaming into their eyes, black-faced at day's end—diggers of the precious yellow gold.

Eighteen-seventy-nine was also the year Daddy went to work at the Standard Mine at the famous Bodie Bluffs. Oh, I know that name so well! When I was a small child, the word "Standard" was almost up with God himself! Daddy was so proud of the work that was being done there—I heard over and over every detail of the rock being stuck, how deep it was, the condition of the air, and the need for more timber. It was all Daddy would talk of.

Other men respected my daddy, and not only his Irish countrymen, but also the other miners—they looked to him for good cheer, and for counsel in times of difficulties. Such is the way of the miners who walk together to the top of deep black mines and drop downward on a miniscule platform—down, down into the belly of the earth where they found the gold-bearing quartz, blasting it out and digging it loose with their brawn, hauling it up to the air to be pounded by the great stamping mills, and finally melting it into precious shipments of golden wealth for the owners.

Our cabin was high above the main camp of Bodie—and we had an all-around view of that awesome land.

We lived in a cabin crowded together with other small miners' cabins and those of folks of various laboring trades: wood haulers, mule skinners, carpenters, or iron workers, and others more desperate, and who are always looking for work. It is not fancy, but it smelled of home.

After working all day long, Daddy would come home to us after the winter sun was long put to bed. If my sister Mary and I had already been put to bed, Daddy would always stop in for a good-night kiss. He would rub the stubble of his whiskers on my cheek and tease me: "What me darling, you won't give your daddy a kiss after he has worked so hard for you?"

Sometimes he also smelled of his evening with his brother miners, but my daddy was an honest, God-fearing man, and he never came home stumbling like I would see the single men do so often in the twilight.

My childhood in Bodie is a cloudy jumble: the smell of sage on a hot, breezeless summer day, the brisk feel of walking to school with my sister in the fall, and many things that are lost to me. My sister Mary, three years older than me, started off to school first. I remember Mummy getting Mary up very early in the dim cabin, lit with a single lantern, and dressing her up in whatever layers the weather demanded—a simple cotton dress with an over-apron in the hot, bright days of August; mittens, overcoat, and woolen stockings as November passed to December and the weather turned frigid.

My daddy was sweetness itself, but he spent almost all his life, as I sadly remember, underground in the mines. Most of his above-ground time he spent with "his brothers," whom for years, I actually thought were *our* family, the same as Mary and me.

The too-short moments with us were terribly precious and were often spent at the Miners Union Hall. There, we shared tragedies, holidays, and religious services with fathers and mothers, bachelors and single ladies, children of the mining brotherhood, living as almost a single breathing being, gasping in the dry, thin air of our high mountain home in Bodie.

Standard Mill, rebuilt after the original building burned down 1899
(Photo by Author)

Lively Times in Bodie

Main street has presented a lively sight during the past week. The weather has been all that could be asked for, and outdoor work has been pushed in every direction. The stores, shops, and saloons, have been doing a big trade, especially in the last five days, with nearly seventy thousand dollars in miners' wages circulating around. Wagons long trains and stages arriving daily with freight and passengers; interesting crowds eagerly discussing the latest strike, or some new discovery; capitalists and prospectors joining forces, or driving quick, business-like bargains; the rush and the stir of superintendents hurrying their winter supplies to safe and convenient shelter while the favorable weather lasts; all these are sights and sounds of a prosperous, growing mining town on a solid, substantial basis.

–The Bodie Standard
December 12, 1877
Bodie

Bodie has a population of 1,500, about six hundred of whom are out of employment, and of the latter number not over 250 would work could they find work to do. There are in the town seventeen saloons, five stores, two livery stables, six restaurants, one newspaper, four barber shops, two butcher shops, one fruit store, four lodging houses, two boot shops, one tin shop, one jewelry store, one saddle shop, two drug stores, three doctors,, four lawyers, post office, express office, fifteen houses of ill fame, one bakery, two blacksmith shops, two lumber yards, two daily stage lines, the usual secret societies, and a miners' union. Lots are worth from $100 to $1000. Lumber sells for $70-$100 per thousand feet. There are six or seven good mines and about 700 locations for mines...

–Letter published in the Reno Evening Gazette

Feb. 20, 1878

Bodie

The town of Bodie is situated on a flat, said to be two thousand feet higher than Mount Davidson. God knows it is high enough for me! The flat is about two miles in length by half a mile width, and contains about 175 or 180 houses and cabins. All classes of business is represented...

–Written by a correspondent for the Territorial Virginia Enterprise, Virginia City, *Nevada*

March 1878

Pay Day

By Alex Beck

To-morrow, that good day, is near,

Judy Daniel

When all the boys are of good cheer,
And friendly drink their glass of beer,
On Pay Day.
We are up and ready at sunrise,
To hoist our flag up to the skies,
On Bodie winds it nimbly flies
On Pay Day.
We'll meet our friends and take them in
And help them to a glass of gin,
You bet your boots we've got the tin
On Pay Day.
If we should get a little full,
And take each other by the wool,
Next day we will apologize in full
For Pay Day.
Some say we walk off with our check,
And fill ourselves up to our neck,
And make ourselves a total wreck
On Pay Day.
But don't you think they judge too far?
For great men patronize the bar
And closely hug their little jar,
Without a Pay Day.
December 4, 1877
The Bodie Standard
December 1877

PAY DAY—The Standard paid out 39,000; the Red Cloud,
Black Hawk, Bechel, McClinton, Bodie, Bulwer, and other
mines of less fame, from $25,000 to $30,000.
–The Bodie Standard
Dec. 12, 1877

The miners of Bodie met last Monday evening for the purpose of organizing a miners' union, but adjourned until the second Tuesday in January when they will effect a permanent organization and elect officers for the ensuing year.

The Bodie Standard

Jan. 3, 1878

Miners' Wages

It occurred to the San Francisco Alta [newspaper] a few days ago to mournfully remark "Most of the quartz mines of Amador, Placer, and Nevada counties are either closed down or unprofitable because of high wages...Quartz mining is crippled by the demand of $4.00 per day for the miners...Miners can work for $2.00 per day".

We have a little story to tell the Alta: It is true that the Amador, Placer, and Nevada counties where quartz mining languishes, "first hands" receive only $3.00 per day in the mines and "second hands" receive only $2.50. It is equally true that in Storey county, Nevada, and Mono County, California—the two greatest mining counties on the coast—where quartz mining does not languish but is profitable and increasing in importance miners all receive 4.00 per day...does the Alta not know that in most mining towns day board is $8.00 per week; that night lodgings cost from $15.00 to $25.00 per month; that a suit of clothes for a miner, bought in a mining town, costs as much as the Alta man himself? Does he want the miner to do without even the comforts of life—to say nothing of luxury? Shall the miner do without books and papers; without the occasional day of rest or pleasure trip? No!

When we hear a mining camp complain that its ledges remain undeveloped owing to the high price of labor, we at once suspect that there are other and better causes for neglect. The mining men who pay high wages are never heard to complain. Let miners' wages remain at their present figure. We want no Chinamen, or Kearneyites and "labor agitation" here in the mountains.

The Bodie Standard

Jan. 9, 1878

A Donation—Monday William H. Dolman donated a lot on Main street, south of Green street, 35x100 feet to the Bodie Miners' Union. An eligible lot, that.

The Bodie Standard

May 15, 1878

Sketch by Author

Miners' Union Hall—This new hall, on which work was commenced less than a week ago, is now being rapidly erected. The sides are up and the floor is laid, and it will be completed before the 28th of this month. The building is 30x70 feet and *has two ante rooms in the front 10x12, and the hall will be 12 feet high. The front will be handsomely finished and when completed will cost $8000 and be quite an addition to this town.*

–The Bodie Standard
May 1878

Hall of Bodie Miners' Union, Bodie, July 9, 1878—The members of this organization are hereby notified that the funeral of our deceased brother EDWARD COX will take place WEDNESDAY AFTERNOON at 3 o'clock, from the Bodie Miners' Union Hall. Members and friends of the deceased are invited to attend.

–The Bodie Standard
July 11, 1878

The funeral of Alex Nixon

The late Alex Nixon, who was shot and killed by Thomas McDonald on the morning of June 13th, was buried from the hall of the Bodie Miners' Union Friday evening.. At 3:30 the Miners' Union formed in line and the funeral cortege moved off. The number of Union men was about one hundred, and there was besides one hundred and fifty citizens in the procession. It was probably one of the largest turn-outs ever seen in Bodie.

–The Bodie Standard
June 1878

Mary, of course, had the more difficult position; since I was the baby of the family, she had the chore of watching out for me. Mary had to get me up and dressed, and make sure my face and hands were cleaned. Daddy was long gone (oh, I was always so disappointed!) when we came to the table for our morning meal. After our meal, Mary made sure my apron was straightened and my warm cap was on my head before we walked off to school.

Mary carried our lunch in an old lard tin Mummy had cleaned out, and Daddy had found an old leather strap to make a handle—I guess I could not be trusted not to sneak a bite! I had to always go to Mary at the lunch bell, and she would very fairly split our bit of bread, gravy, and whatever small bite Mummy could spare of the family food.

After lunch, we always had a time for play while the teachers ate their own lunches, inside the school. In most weathers, we children were expected to be outside to get our "air" and "exercise." We studied the line to the outdoor privies to make sure we spent the least amount of time there away from playing tag and telling secrets. Mary, being older, always sat with her girlfriends and shared paper dolls, or letters they were writing, or did a bit of sewing while discussing important older girl things. Mary's job was to mind me as I frolicked with the others my age, and was at me constantly to "mind not to dirty my dress" or tear my apron, and to not lose my mittens as I would surely be reprimanded. It was my job to run about, throw rocks in Bodie Creek, and never listen to Mary's worry about dirtying my dress—Mummy surely could wash and mend it!

Bodie Creek, below the Green Street Schoolhouse
(Photo by Author)

Mummy had no life of luxury living in the harsh climate of Bodie, in a cramped cabin that let in the winter cold and the summer's sweltering heat. Of course, Mummy always thought she had the best life that a woman could expect, with Daddy always in steady work and with her own house—many of the families back home in Ireland would think we lived in absolute paradise, as we had plenty of food to eat and we children went to school and not to work every day. Mummy did not have Daddy's sunny smile and laugh, but she had a quiet, solemn manner that told the world hers was a life to be envied—married with children and living in a free country.

Mummy's day began before Daddy went off into the darkness, as she had to stoke the breakfast fire for the porridge and pack Daddy's lunch of cold potatoes and bacon-greased bread. His clothing must be laid out, his boots cleaned up, and the lamps set out and ready to light the first time. Mummy took great pride in her household chores, and other than a priest to say Mass every Sunday, she seemed to have no other desires.

On Mondays, Mummy baked the week's bread, setting out the rising bowl. It was the most valuable piece of crockery in our home, and something us girls never even so much as looked at, let alone touched. In the cold winters, Mummy had to pray over her stubborn rising dough, and kneading it was enough to leave Mummy huffing. But oh, the smells that surrounded us on Mondays are something that just makes my mouth water even to this day. Daddy always seemed to hurry home for Monday's evening meal, since of course the first slice was always his, then Mary's, then mine, and always last, Mummy's. After school, Mary again must gather the now-empty lunch tin, see to my coat and cap, and then, saying a fond farewell to her best friend, walk me back up the hill to our house, where she must again wash my face and hands, straighten up my apron, and sit with me at the kitchen table to do sums and read aloud. Most important was to not disturb Mummy, who was getting Daddy's supper ready. In fine weather, I could talk Mary into some dallying on the way home, to gather bits of wildflowers to decorate our table and make up stories about what kinds of lives we might live when we became grown-ups. Lots of times Mary had to hurry to the house to help Mummy with the folding, ironing, and dusting, and no amount of teasing about a certain boy who always seemed to be looking her way could distract my good sister from her chores. My chore was always sweeping the back stoop, and perhaps shoveling dirt on the stove ashes so it would not blow right back inside. It was a good job for me because it could always be blamed for why my dress was so much grimier than Mary's, and lots of days I volunteered to do it before I even stepped inside, so Mummy did not see how lunchtime had been too much fun. Mary always raised her brow at me and told me I should make sure to tell the priest my bit of deceiving, though somehow I seemed to forget by Saturday. Mary always was just like Mummy, and I had that bit of Daddy in me.

Tuesdays, Mummy had to heat up water to launder all the clothing, and the cleaning of the ever-present black grit of the miner's overall was no easy task. Mummy always blessed our modern times—she could purchase a bit of pre-made soap, even on our family's tight budget. Each time she would use it, she would smile, soaking and stirring our clothing, wringing it out by hand, and in summer,

Children's Dress

In the 1870s and 1880s, all girls exclusively wore dresses.

With the advent of new synthetic dyes, the clothes children wore started to be more colorful. Plaids and stripes became popular. Often these were so favored by the wearers that the bold patterns would seem mismatched to the modern eye.

Braiding and trims became more popular, and as women's fashions were the model for girls' dresses, the sleeves might puff a bit, or have bits of ribbons sewn on them if they were full-length.

Starch came into popular usage, and the over-pinafore was often religiously ironed to be quite stiff for our modern tastes. The daily over-the-dress apron was a bit shorter than the dress, and might have a bit of ruffle at the sleeveless yoke.

Some girls began to wear "Roman sandals," which we call now the Mary Jane, most probably to special events, as the ankle button-up boot was still the standard of excellence for walking in the dust of summer and the mud of all the other seasons of Bodie.

Full-length dark or striped cotton or woolen stockings were always worn, as were several layers of white cotton undergarments, including a small undershirt and the obligatory pantaloon.

Girls now wore a beret- style wool cap in winter, often decorated with a wool decorative yarn ball. Short brim straw hats were popular for special events and summertime, but all girls wore a hat outdoors. Capes were still common, but the wool jacket was being worn by children who could afford this new style. Often the jacket and cape were combined to allow several seasons of growing room.

drying out in the sage-scented airs. In winter it decorated our front room close to the iron stove that heated our home.

Wednesday was sewing and mending day. Since she handmade all of our clothes, this was a constant business. Daddy's work pants were the modern ones, purchased at the emporium along with his boots, but pants needed mending, socks must be darned, and shirts sewn. The fancier folks now seemed to purchase all their family clothing from the stores of Bodic, brought up from San Francisco. But Mummy took time with our clothing, and Mary and I were lucky to always show well-tailored and clean clothing, since not all the children had this tender care.

Thursday was the day the house got a thorough cleaning—not just the simple straightening that happened every day. In good weather, rugs were lifted to the rope line outdoors and beaten with a wooden paddle. The fireplace was totally swept out and the ashes buried out back of the house. The curtains were shaken out. The lamps were filled with kerosene and the wicks tended and trimmed. The floors were scrubbed on hand and knee, and Mummy's hands would be very red and almost swollen when she finished. The soot was cleaned off the inside of the few windows we had, and in summertime the outsides were given a scrubbing as well.

Friday being payday, all the tradesmen knew that Daddy's credits were to be paid. Mummy would haggle with the butcher and look thoughtfully at the bin of potatoes, always trying to pick up a special blend of tobacco that Daddy smoked in his pipe. The necessities of the household were shrewdly purchased and some things were left out if Daddy needed his boots resoled—an added expense—and this shopping and budgeting took Mummy quite a bit of time. Sometimes the other miners' wives were on the same quests. Medical advice was exchanged and children praised for a good report, and even a bit of gossip might be heard. Anyway, Mummy always took all the morning on Fridays with this business and was always in a rush to get back to prepare Daddy's supper.

After the two of us girls went up to bed, Mummy and Daddy would sit together, quietly, in the dying moments of their day. Daddy would always tease Mummy about her Friday business, and would try to get her to share what the other wives had repeated to her in the strictest confidence—I guess I never did know if Mummy did tell. In front of me, Mummy never told, but maybe after my bedtime, stories were shared.

And finally, Saturday! This was always my favorite of days, because Daddy only worked until our noon meal and we would, in fine weather, often pack up our good bread with a bit of cold meat or fruits and take a family picnic. Often other miners' families would join us along the shady willows of the lower creek lands along Cottonwood Canyon, and the parents would relax on a blanket in the meadow grasses. We children were allowed to run freely from family to family and share bits of candy treats or peaches.

One time we had real ice cream! It was made up for us by one of the new merchants trying to drum up new business.

If we didn't picnic, we girls were walked and shown off in the town, while Daddy went to all of the shops and paid his bills. We could window shop and make up fantastic lists of things we would buy in the future, and for sure we always got a

Bodie Market Report

Flour—$1.50 per pound.

Oatmeal—10-121/4 c per lb.

Buckwheat—121/2to 15c per lb.

Potatoes—6 to 8c per lb.

Beans—10121/4c per lb.

Cabbage—8c per lb.

Onions—8c per lb.

Turnips—8c per lb.

Fruit—apples,green8 to 121/4c per lb. pears ,dried 16 to 20c per lb.—can $4-5 per doz.

Sugar—crushed 20c;granulated 221/4c per 1 lb. in boxes.

Coffee—green30-40c per lb.

Tea 50c to $1.50 per lb.

Coal oil—$1-$1.25 per gal.

Candles—$1.50per box of 20lb.

Butter—371/2 to 45c:roll

Cheese—California, 25 to 371/2c per lb.

Eggs—75c per dozen

Honey-comb,30c per lb.

Beef—10 to 25c per lb.

Pork—25c per lb.

Mutton—121/2 to 15c per lb.
Veal—121/2 to 25c per lb.
Ham—California, 231/2 to 25c per lb.
Bacon—20-25c per lb.
Wood $14.50 per cord.
The Chronicle
Dec. 28, 1878

Bodie Window View
(Photo by Author)

    few pennies' worth of hard candy to share fairly between Mummy, Daddy, and we two lucky girls.

    Back home, neighbors would stop by, and sometimes the checkerboard came out, and the men would let us watch as they bet rocks and twigs on the games. I heard the rocks and twigs were traded for glasses of brew at the pubs later in the evening, but I never went inside a pub, so I don't know for sure.

Sunday was Mass day, which was the highlight of Mummy's week, but for Mary and me a chance to break in new shoes or wear that little hat, perhaps even with a ribbon in my hair.

For some time, I remember the father saying Mass at the Union Hall, sandwiched between the minister saying his services. People of all faiths shared the brotherhood of the Union Hall. But mostly I remember our little Catholic church over on the end of Fuller Street at the very entrance of Main Street. St. John the Baptist Catholic Church stood at the head of our town. Even though in later years it was completely lost in a big fire, this little building shared many moments with our family. It was the day Daddy always wore real pants with a freshly pressed shirt, a corduroy coat, and a cap, which he, of course, respectfully took off inside the church and put in his coat pocket.

Mummy carefully brushed off her best dress. It was dark brown silk and trimmed in black velvet ribbon. Her little button hat was pinned over her braids. A little jewel-pin that had been her own mummy's was stuck close to her heart, and always shined there like a little star. It brought her warm memories of her own childhood back in Ireland.

After Mass, the families would sip tea or coffee that the Ladies Society fixed up. Bits of pastry would often be displayed on long tables covered in freshly-laundered lace.

A bowl was set out on these tables, where families would give a coin or two if they could. But everyone was welcome to partake, even those in hard times who didn't have a coin to drop in.

Celebration of the Fourth of July, 1878

For several days preceding the Fourth, the wind was very high and for a time it was feared that the weather would prevent a full turnout, but early Wednesday evening the wind subsided and Thursday morning the sun rose from behind the hills beautiful and bright, and the people of Bodie were aroused from their peaceful slumbers by the firing of thirteen guns...The whole length of Main street there was almost one continuous line of streamers...At 10:30 A.M. the procession formed near Miners' Union Hall, and marched down Main Street...The Day closed with the Miners' Union Ball...Early in the evening the guest commenced arriving and it was not long before the handsome hall was crowded. From Aurora, Bridgeport, and all over this section they came, intent upon having a splendid time.

–The Bodie Standard
July 6, 1878

Loaf Cake—Two cups light dough, one cup sugar, half cup butter, two eggs, half teaspoon soda, one cup raisins, and spice to suit your taste.

–The Chronicle
Dec. 28, 1878

Bread Pudding
Stale bread, milk, 3 eggs, pinch of salt, cinnamon, 1 teaspoon molasses, raisins.

Crumble the bread the night before you want to serve it and soak overnight in milk. Next beat the eggs with the bread and a little salt. Tie it up in a bag, or in a pan that will exclude every drop of water. Boil it about an hour or a little more. When tied in a bag, no pudding should be put into the pot till the water boils.

Georgianne Bowman, 1860s Foods on the Frontier, Courtesy of the North Carolina Historical Society, www. buffnet.net/macdowel/cross/recipes.htm

Potato Soup

1 quart potatoes, peeled and cubed, 1 ½ quarts stock, 1 cup stale bread crumbs, carrot and or celery if available: Place the potatoes, carrots, and celery in a soup pot with one quart of stock; cook, covered , for ten minutes or until the potatoes are soft. Add the bread and cook ten minutes longer, then add the remainder of the stock. Season to your taste.

1860s Foods on the Frontier

This was the widow's fund, to help the families of miners who went into work

but never came home. I, for one, held a terror in my heart seeing the bowl fill with coins and thinking of my own daddy not coming home. But Daddy seemed to know my fear of this donation bowl and he would always quietly take my hand and squeeze it firmly and I knew, not my daddy. He would always come home to me.

After the coffee was cold we would amble back to the house. Then many of the miners would drop in while the women were all busy cooking the big meal for the week. They were checking to see that the potatoes and cabbage were just so, and every bit of meat, whether mutton, beef, or rarely, chicken, was completely cooked, and all the drippings saved for gravy.

In good times a bit of dessert was also prepared, perhaps a mincemeat pie or a tart in fruit season. We girls always knew the family finances when we sat down to Sunday supper; desserts only came out in flush times. When finances were tight even the greens would be forgone and we might be reduced to a bit of meat and gravy with bread, and Daddy always served first and most.

My daddy was always the gentleman. Our children's meal might be slighted, but he insisted Mummy serve herself an equal portion to his, no matter Mummy's quiet protest that she was still full from the church breakfast.

Sometimes I saw Mummy put hers aside when Daddy had already got up to go to light his after-dinner pipe, and her portion looked a lot like Monday's bubble and squeak that we all enjoyed next evening with our freshly-baked bread.

After the night fell on Sunday, the men would again appear, and there could be loud talk of the doings at the mines and the union meetings, and I would often smell the sweet tang of whiskey in the air. Mummy never sat in on these meetings—men's business, she called it. She would suddenly swoosh us up to our bedrooms and comb Mary's beautiful long hair, and sometimes tell stories of her girlhood as she braided Mary's freshly combed hair. My hair was never long enough for braids that held, and so Mummy would trim my fringe and fluff up my curls. "Daddy's hair," she called it with a smile. It was our one special time that Mummy sat with us, so that Daddy could sit with his brother miners, sometimes until the wee hours, depending on what the mining operations called for.

CHAPTER SIX:

TURKEYS AND OYSTERS:

"JUST ENOUGH TO BE COMFORTABLE"

Mono County was created by an act of the Legislature on April 21, 1861, and was the first of the mining counties to be organized as such on the Eastern slope of the Sierra Nevada mountains...Mono County averages 108 miles in length and average width...is thirty-eight miles...3,030 square miles...the land is rough, mountainous and spectacular...the town of Bodie is located seven miles south and thirteen miles east of the town of Bridgeport, the County seat.

www.monocounty.ca.gov

> *Mono County has 7,100 people; just enough to be comfortable.*
> *–The Daily Free Press*
> *Jan. 11, 1881*

Another Growl—San Francisco and Sacramento have been growling because the census enumerators have not footed up a population equal to what has been claimed for them by their papers. And now comes Bodie a growling, the census taker giving us a population of only 5,417, when we have been claiming from seven thousand to ten thousand people in our altitudinous burg. Perhaps our enumerators have omitted a few, but is not 5,416 a goodly population for a place that may be said to be really only about two years old? We think it is.

—The Bodie Standard
July 1880

San Francisco in 1880 recorded approximately 234,223 persons, Virginia City had 9,427 persons, Reno had 6,434 persons, Carson City had 5,109 persons, Bodie had 5,272 persons, Bridgeport had 827 persons, and Genoa had 312 persons.

—1880 United States Federal Census.

My life as the girl, Helen Anne Kernohan, had come to flower. I took graduation with no little sadness, as I had grown fond of the spelling bees and the mathematics, and quite enjoyed geography. I was chosen to read a parting poem aloud, as was the tradition to my classmates, as all of Bodie crowded into the new Green Street schoolhouse. My mother and her husband, Mr. Huntoon, both had tears of pride as I walked across the room to take my formal diploma from the high school at Bodie. Uncle Ben cheered, and Uncle Wilson Butler handed me a new pen and stationary set as soon as I rejoined my family. I was Helen Anne Kernohan, scholar. I felt like the whole world was mine.

Mother said an education like mine will make a great difference. I would be ready to make my way, using my skills in writing and calculating figures, not just her skills in wringing out soiled skirts or cooking for others. Mr. Huntoon hid a knowing smile. This was an argument no one would take up with Mother, even though the menfolk saw that times were changing.

Times did change for our family. No longer bound by school, Mr. Sawyer stepped forward as soon as was proper and courted me to become his bride. On April 6, 1879, I answered him in front of my entire family that I was ready to take the next step and open a new chapter as wife and mother.

Mr. Sawyer was well known to my Bodie family, as he had worked in the dairy business with Mr. Huntoon, my stepfather. And like the rest of our mixed clan of Butlers, Kernohans, and Huntoons, Mr. Sawyer had a vision for our Bodie. Just as my mother saw that a new type of lodging was desperately needed for all of the important visitors, skilled tradesmen, and mining experts, my new husband was ready to jump in and make this happen. We talked for hours about the future Booker Flats Hotel, Livery, Saloon, and Eatery. It was an exciting time and all of us canvassed our skills and offered what we thought was needed. Mr. Sawyer would run the saloon, and help out if needed with the guest's horses and carriages. Uncle Will could repair any wagon folks might have, shoe their horses, and help Mother set up a large kitchen with a bigger stove. Mr. Huntoon was to be manager, and I was chosen to help run the front areas and keep books. My school days would pay off, and I would dress as the lady Mother wanted. Uncle Ben would supply our firewood needs, and his two boys would also be involved, helping with chores and running errands. Of course, for such a big venture, capital for the building would be needed, and Mr. Huntoon went visiting his many associates in Bridgeport. Many of these longtime neighbors decided to loan Mr. Huntoon the funds we needed to start.

My husband and I began our married life much as I had lived all my life. Mother had several rooms to let for paying boarders at the Cottonwood Valley farmhouse, and my husband and I leased one of these until better times would bring us a house of our own.

In June 1880, it was time to take the decennial census in Bodie. Advertisements were placed in the newspaper for men to canvass the town, and several men were hired. Over a week to ten days, they were expected to hand-write all the names and other information received from all of the township of Bodie. At that time, it was not really known what the true population was. Some were surprised at the final tally of 5,417 individuals, thinking our town was surely ten thousand at least.

I became involved in this census in an unusual way. One of the enumerators was boarding at the farm house, a Mr. Johnson.

This man was a very serious fellow, with a long-suffering concern regarding his spectacles. We heard of his malaise at every meal-time. He truly got worked up, worrying he would surely be let go if the others knew he could but barely see the pages of the big census book. He was supposed to be writing down all of the daily totals all the other counters gathered each evening onto the final pages. Mother, of course, felt concerned for him, what with his eyes just getting redder by the hour, but being the problem solver she was, came up with a good plan. Why, every evening, Mr. Johnson could sit in her very roomy kitchen, and her young scholar of a daughter, newly-married and in truth in need of some spare cash, could write out the day's figures.

Mr. Johnson was in doubt at first that a young lady's penmanship could ever be up to such a lofty endeavor as the United States Census. But mother's persuasiveness is renowned, and Mr. Johnson needed the paycheck for his own distant family. So I wrote out the figures and facts Mr. Johnson gathered each day, and his colleagues never guessed it was a young lady who did the handwriting.

Some folks were out of town during that period. Because we lived in Bodie and had a large group of acquaintances, we had a different view than the enumerators. Why take, for example, that young James and Martha Cain, with whom I was acquainted because we shared a butcher. These two were in Carson City celebrating the arrival of their first child. The infant David Victor Cain was counted in the Carson census, but not his parents. After a strict stare from Mr. Johnson on the first evening of our partnership, I realized information like this was not to be discussed. Mr. Johnson and his fellows were strictly counting who was present. If they were not in town for whatever reason, they didn't make the tally. Mr. Johnson might let a young lady help out, but she had best keep quiet. I settled down and just stuck to the numbers.

We all knew folks that avoided the census-takers on purpose, despite the well-noticed warnings in the newspaper that failure to step forth carried a $100 fine. Ladies of the red-light district appear to have chosen to risk that fine. Paiutes and Chinese may not have been aware of the census itself, or the threat of a fine, because of the language barrier, or more probably because of a natural apprehension of the ways of whites. That doesn't mean all the Chinese and Native Americans were left out, just that their numbers are not in line with what we as insiders knew of their presence.

Perhaps rumors that some "enumerators" chose to settle into a chair in, say, a saloon, and enroll all those present and did not have time to walk about were true. Supervision of the enumerators appears to have been lax, myself doing the scribing a case in point. Seeing as I was involved in this important business, all visitors were sworn to secrecy, but enjoyed sharing stories about the mannerisms and work ethic of the other enumerators, who didn't happen to be boarding with us.

Nonetheless, the work became a milestone in my life. I began to see Bodie in a new light. I began to enjoy the work of grouping businesses, households, boardinghouses, and mining companies. I loved spelling out the names, and listing occupation, place of birth, and seeing who could read and write. The view of Bodie that the census takers recorded of our town was in neat black letters on a white page. We townspeople might have our own thoughts on the real Bodie, but that did not hold water to this work.

The saga of my own uncles, Ben and Wilson, with regard to the census was one we all joked about for years. Most would acknowledge that these two were perhaps the most long-term residents of our fair town. Ben Butler, married, is listed as a wood contractor, grouped among his employees. His children, at ages eight and ten, are listed as being their own household, since they were at that time also living at our farmhouse. The boys had been with us since the unfortunate passing of their mother. So Ben was really a widower, but was labeled married. Uncle Will is another case. Will always went fishing the first week of June with his buddies down to the Glass Creek and June Lake areas. He must have been gone just long enough to be completely left off the final tally, although Wilson is regarded by all as the most senior resident of the area, dating back to the camp days of our town. But you will never know any of this if you are to read that document. As for me, I faithfully scribed what Mr. Johnson asked me to.

So you may wonder, how did the counting in 1880 occur? It seems that the enumerators chose to walk into a business, sit down, and attempt to scribe all the persons in the place at the time. It is easy to see that if one did not happen to be present there, one could be missed.

The list that I received each evening was fascinating to me, and I thought I knew Bodie! Joseph Beck and his wife Margaret are listed, but the two girls, whom I knew well from school, Mary E. and Alice E., are listed as Joseph's children and not Margaret's! I am sure this was a very interesting tidbit that the enumerators got mixed up—but then we all knew the real truth, so what the government received was probably the result of too much time counting in the corner saloon, with, as Mr. Sawyer said, drinks flowing to keep the dust off the pages.

The manner the enumerators used to count the Paiute Indians was very curious to me. Only Captain Bob, the chief, is documented by name. All the other tribe members are simply labeled Paiute 1, Paiute 2, etc. Now, I had been raised with all of these hardworking people since I was a young girl, and I knew their white names—Sally, Sadie, Dick, Tom, etc. I am sure none of us ever knew their real names, as I had learned in school that they had Indian names they did not share. We never had any problems in Bodie with our Paiute neighbors, and we benefited many times when it came to harvest work, or household chores that were too much for a young mother with a baby. But again, not being from Bodie, Mr. Johnson certainly would not understand, and by the time I was writing up these folks, I didn't say a peep. Mother said it wasn't going to do any good to rile up Mr. Johnson's politics.

The Chinese were also a confusing group to count. Although many are listed by name, I surely had great difficulty figuring out what Mr. Johnson scribbled on his bits of papers. We had many Chinese businessmen, and Mr. Johnson seemed to be quite faithful here. I was quite amazed, as these men all seemed to have wives (often they were listed with more than one wife!) We all knew firsthand from the press that King Street was home to many of these celestials, but I for one did not ever recall seeing a respectable woman. I was so disappointed that not one of the Chinese women was listed by name. Chinese children were not on the tally. I had learned at our own Bodie school geography lesson that Chinese culture highly regards the birth of multiple children, and it is was inconceivable to me that Chinese wives of the merchant and trade classes did not bear children in Bodie. But although these concepts seem logical from my educated and modern viewpoint, it remained a fact the enumerators did not count any Chinese children. Mother said possibly these men did not dare go inside the homes on King Street. I felt frustration for these gaps due to my own interest in historical correctness, but I carefully tucked away these views.

When labeling some of the female occupations, Mother cautioned me to not be upset. Mother's sense of morality regarding these ladies was a subject she kept from me. Numerous women were listed as living with no husbands, but nonetheless were discreetly labeled as "keeping house." I assured Mother that as a worldly married lady I was aware that some places in Bodie were the domain of folks the rest of us did not associate with socially. In the 1880 census, all of these single "housewives" had names such as Minnie, Netty, Daisy, Kitty, Mamie, or Maud. That they had real names suggested that these ladies were considered to be a step above the Chinese and the Paiutes. Mother countered that from our stand at the farm, we had many doings with the working Paiutes, and the laundry services of the Chinese, but we never had set a table with the "gay" ladies of Maiden Lane.

Who were the "folks" who lived in Bodie in 1880? And what did these people do to support themselves?

The first name on the list that I hand-copied was Isadore Hyman--single, white, male, born in Poland, age 29. His occupation is listed as "tobacconist." As you may know the census pages had eight to nine columns across and almost fifty spaces down. Each person, regardless of age, got their own numbered line, and each person's age, occupation, married status, relationship to head of household, and real estate holdings was checked off. There was even a question about birthplace, and I admit the number of places around the world I recorded became a source of great interest to our family and we had fun reading these aloud. We felt we were seeing the world from our front porch!

But let's get back to Isadore Hyman, tobacconist; the first Bodie resident I prepared to record. What, I thought was a To-bac-co-nist? I asked my husband as he sat trying to relax after his busy day, and after a bit of pondering he kindly explained: a seller of tobacco products and supplies such as cigarettes, tobacco, and pipes. An old- fashioned title in our modern Bodie!

Surprisingly, this profession supported a total of three men in 1880 Bodie! I would remember this occupation when I was able to read that week's newspaper and saw numerous ads for cigar merchants. Our town evidently was a prosperous place for a tobacconist.

Two weeks was the time allotted for the enumerators to gather their facts, and every evening I was single-minded in getting the lists completed. I knew the penmanship must be my best, and I organized the notes carefully so I would make no errors. I even organized many of the personal data into my own categories, which helped me to do a better job. I became absorbed in the variety of work that the men were able to provide, and I became even more interested to see many adventuresome and upstanding women making a go of things. Mother was also fascinated by the changes that our Bodie was seeing, and it was mainly for her enjoyment that I created a notebook of my own census "statistics." I separated men from women, and had lists of occupations that I labeled "service," "trades," "miners," "professionals," "public officials," and "agriculturalists." Mr. Johnson gathered all the lists from the other scribes and every day brought me lists to ink onto the large pages. The pages would be turned into county and state records to be bound into large volumes. It is these records that would be used to determine state and federal needs for electoral representation in the legislature. Every male counted was a plus for Bodie, as it bolstered our acceptance as a serious contender with other gold towns.

The variety of livelihoods did take me by surprise:

16 Clerks in a store

22 Bartenders

8 Cooks in a Hotel

1 Drug-store clerk

8 Grocers

4 Winers

4 Furniture Dealers

1 News Agent

3 Dry Goods clerks

3 Hardware clerks

1 Express Office clerk

2 Liquor dealers

2 Livery Stable keepers

10 Hotel waiters

1 Clothing Store clerk

1 Livery Stable worker

3 Bank clerks

2 Commercial travelers

3 Peddlers

61 clerks

23 Merchants

1 Bootblack

2 Station-keepers

1 Fruit and Vegetable vender

1 Pub worker

1 Fruit Vender

3 Vegetable grocers

1 Stationer

1 Fish Merchant

1 Chop stand

1 Helper

1 Milkman

1 Ivory Broker

19 Chinese kitchen helpers

5 Chinese dishwashers

7 Chinese storekeepers

8 Chinese domestics

11 Chinese washhouse workers

2 Chinese grocers

1 Chinese druggist

5 Chinese peddlers

1 Chinese lodging housekeeper

26 Chinese laundrymen

Such a variety of skilled tradesmen were counted for Bodie. Growing up around my uncles, I was aware of these handy fellows, but I never realized how much a part of Bodie they had become.

Reading over this list, Mother and I felt pride in our Bodie. Work was available in Bodie for a wide range of skilled men. A much shorter list of 71 men listed "no occupation." Uncle Will thought this was the answer as to how Bodie got such a reputation for wild times, even when almost every able- bodied man seemed to be working like a beaver. His view was, like most towns, we just got used to telling the same tall tales to give us an air of a big city. Hard-working Bodie-ites themselves created the myth of being a wild town, with nightly excitements to be expected on Main Street after dark. As for Bodie being a gun fighters' capital, full of bad men? Why that was just newspaper men putting a glamorous spin on a few misunderstandings. It was an inside joke they were all in on. Then time just clouded the reality, and the tall tale was more fun to tell.

Bodie Window
(Photo by Author)

5 clothiers	6 boot makers
5 upholsterers	475 laborers/not married
76 laborers/married	8 tailors
2 pressmen	11 painters
127 carpenters	17 tinsmiths
7 stonemasons	117 teamsters
77 blacksmiths	209 woodchoppers
3 boiler makers	18 machinists
15 printers	12 shoemakers
2 paper hangers	2 stonemen

6 bakers

1 gas fitter

10 amalgamators

1 timber man in mines

1 pattern maker

5 Chinese teamsters

2 firemen

9 Chinese wood haulers

7 harness makers

1 wagonmaker

1 amalgamator in quartz mill

3 brewers

3 wood dealers

4 brick layers

5 foremen

5 iron workers

27 wood packers

4 barbers

6 mill hands

1 undertaker

1 locksmith

1 timekeeper

2 wood haulers

57 mill men

1 rounder

2 tinners

1 stager

3 packers

1 ice manufacturer

7 tailors

12 engine firemen

2 boot makers

2 freighters

1 confectioner

1 mason

19 Chinese laborers

1 farm-implement maker

4 shoe shop workers

1 hostler

4 contractors

1 house mover

3 wheelwrights

1 drayman

1 foundry

1 draughtsman

1 merchant tailor

4 mechanics

15 prospectors

1 lumber dealer

1 plasterer

1 wood contractor

1 millwright

1 stage driver

1 pump man

2 jockeys

1 water dealer

2 soda water manufacturers

1 carver

Many of these skills men of Bodie puzzled me as to what they really did all day. I had to look up several in the dictionary or ask my husband Mr. Sawyer if he knew what they were. Here are some of the explanations I found:

Amalgamate: alloy with mercury: to alloy a metal with mercury.

Brew: to make beer or similar alcoholic drinks by a process of steeping, boiling, and fermenting grain with hops, sugar, and other ingredients.

Clerk: service desk worker, general office worker, same as sales clerk.

Dray(man): a cart without sides: a large low horse-drawn cart with no fixed sides, designed for heavy loads.

Foreman: a man in charge of other workers.

Foundry: workplace for casting metal or glass: making castings (of metal or glass).

Harness maker: a person who makes a set of leather straps fitted to an animal such as a horse so that it can be attached to a cart or carriage for pulling.

Hostler: engineer: somebody employed to service a large vehicle such as a locomotive: horse minder: formerly, someone employed to take care of horses at an inn.

Millwright: somebody who designs, builds, or maintains mills or mill machinery.

Undertaker: somebody whose profession is to prepare the dead for burial, and to arrange funerals

Wheelwright: A skilled worker in both wood and iron, somebody who makes and repairs wheels, especially the wheels of carriages and wagons.

Window shot, Bodie by the author

One of the trades was listed as "house mover." This was Mr. F.C. Houghton, who was well known in Bodie! You don't just but wonder how much work he did, but many stories abound about "used buildings." These structures were built for one purpose, failed at that and were then bought and up and moved, with some other function giving the wooden framework new life. Wood was scarce, and skilled labor to build was also very valuable, so buildings were often less expensive to move than to build. Most of the structures that were built were simple wood boxes, and thinking of them in this light helped me understand why moving a building made good sense. Many cabins moved from camp to camp—from Monoville to Aurora and then to Bodie. We thought it grand that our Bodie was so quick to make a good use of old hopes.

The schoolhouse that stands today on Green Street actually used to be a lodging house on Main Street. Another of Bodie's buildings was sold to be a schoolhouse for an adjoining town in northerly Antelope Valley.

The real core of Bodie would always be the work done in and around the mines up on the Bluff. Uncle Ben had many business dealings with big mining companies, and he delighted in congratulating the Butler clan for the good sense in picking out Bodie to settle in. The statistics on the mining operations are truly amazing! What we found in 1880 rosters were 582 single, male miners between the ages of fifteen and twenty-nine years; 590 single, male miners between thirty and 40 years, and 145 single, male miners over the age of forty, the oldest being sixty-two years of age! That is a total of *one thousand three hundred and seventeen single men!* These men worked ten-hour shifts, six days a week. At four dollars a day, thanks to the strong Miner's Union of Bodie, these were the highest wages paid to skilled men in our state.

In addition, there were *225 married miners* whose wives did **not** live in Bodie in 1880. All of these men lived in the lodging houses that most often included room and family-style board. Some of the big mines found it feasible to build and service their own boardinghouses. The Syndicate Mine did this. Other men without wives would room together in bachelor quarters, and relied upon the weekly board provided at the plentiful eating establishments. Most saloons had chophouses (fast-food grills) attached to the bar, so a fellow could drink his daily brew and then grab a bite before drifting back to his bunk.

A fewer number, ninety-nine in total, were miners who lived with their wives in Bodie, usually with several children as well. Joseph Beck, who was well known to all of us, was one of these. Ben felt this singled Joe Beck out as one of those who planned to make Bodie their home, in addition to their livelihood. If a miner was married with a family, most often he invested in one of the very small box miner's cabins; either renting or purchasing through the bank. These miners were the backbone of the mining success of our town, and were held in high regard among all our citizens.

The list of miners' names helped Mother and I realize that the Bodie mining operations are composed of American citizens from every state, as well as a variety of European immigrants. Each man was some mother's son, each with a home far from Bodie, all present to take a part in the skilled labor the dark and dangerous mine offered.

One puzzling exception was one house of seven immigrants that all had good

Author's note: When Mr. Almond Huntoon lost his land to his creditors, his Booker Flats Hotel was moved all the way to his brother, Mr. Sidney Huntoon's, property at Rickey's Station, a distance of possibly twenty miles. Just imagine the logistics of moving a large multi-room building down the rough dirt roads of the 1880s; it must have made quite a sight.

Even the famous James Cain House of today's Bodie was moved from a location up Green Street, near the school, to where it stands today, across from what is today labeled the David Cain house on Green and Park Streets. The original builder of this house is the very talented carpenter, Jesse McGath, and was the home of his second wife, our old friend Elizabeth (Butler Kernohan Huntoon) McGath. Ella Cain reports in her writings that Jim Cain jokingly threatened not to pay the house mover "'cause the guy didn't transplant the well" with the house.

Bodie (author's photo)

When great fires struck Bodie, especially the 1892 fire, many of the outlying and unburned houses were moved to the center of town to accommodate folks who had lost their homes and businesses. All this house moving just boggles my imagination, as it seemed a great deal of effort, but a bit of the story becomes easier to understand when it was reported that the Bodie snow was often employed to slide the houses on whole rolling timbers pulled by teams of horses like a giant sleigh across the ground to the new locations.

Irish names, but were listed as of the *Chinese* race! Was this a joke or just a group of Chinese masquerading as Irishmen? Or had too many brews mixed up the enumerator's pen, as Mr. Sawyer seemed to think most likely?

The overwhelming number of unmarried miners is perhaps the answer to the wild reputation of Bodie; that many single hardworking men in one small high altitude town would definitely need to let off steam somehow, and the saloons (fifty-four listed as a main business) and dancing establishments were just waiting for the shift whistle to blow. Respectable women such as Mother, I, and our circle did not venture into this Bodie, but no one denies that it was there.

Bodie was also well-represented by a large professional class, who, with one notable exception, which I shall save for last, were *all* men.

Bodie also had public servants, one or two men of the cloth, and members of the agricultural occupations—all men.

I did struggle to categorize the occupations of 1880 Bodie, and whether they were labeled "service," "trade," "professional," "public servant" etc., is merely my whim. I was trying to organize the occupations as a way for me to get a good look at the ways Bodie had changed since the old days. Some felt the engineers were more of a trade, but I felt that the professionals were probably the most literate and educated, and so the engineers were placed in that category, though they could have easily been grouped with the trades.

Author' note: The fact that all the professions excepting one are held by men highlights the historical domination of higher education by males. Since women were not admitted to the means of achieving skills that professionals require, they were not able to compete. In California and the western United States, the placement of women in meaningful work outside the home was making small inroads, beginning first with women attaining college degrees.

Bodie 1880 Professionals

6 Accountants, 3 Lawyers, as opposed to, 11 Attorneys at Law
(Patrick Reddy, the famous defender of the underdog is listed here);
1 Mining Recorder (George MacCarthy), 10 Assayers, 2 gentlemen labeled as Bank Manager, 2 Artists
13 Physicians (D L Deal, Wm Rodgers, Nathan Rodgers, T J Blackwood, GM Summers, J F Summers, H J Roe, David Walker, H D Robertson (actually counted twice), J W Van Zandt, A Anderson);
80 Engineers (which in the lingo of the times may mean the man who *ran* the engines or could mean the man who was *educated* to design, build and keep the big machines operating);
1 Quartz Mill Superintendent; 10 Civil Engineers;
18 Mine Superintendents (Thomas Steele, HA Gould, PA Oliver, SW Blasdell, JB Wood, JNO Boxtrum, Louis Lagrange, DC Norton, WM Irwin, AM Ellsworth, WP

Holmes, Mr. Ferguson, David Moore, JA Graham to name some of this distinguished group);

1 Agent for the transportation company;

2 Photographers (Frank Struckman, age 23, single, and Iver Boyson, age 22, single);

2 clerks at the mine (one of whom, Alex Beck, is often mentioned in the press as a good fellow!),

6 Druggists (Henry Wright, Herbert Fentiss, WA Miller, A Weber, AB Stewart, RI Van Voohees);

4 Surveyors;   6 Real Estate agents;

2 Mining experts (A Morgan, Wm Bradford);   1 Debt Assessor,

1 Collector,   4 Canvassers

1 25-year-old Telegraph Operator, EG Taylor ;

9 Stock Speculators;

11 men who gave their profession as "Gentleman"

1 Auctioneer (30 years, married, PW Smith);

1 Solicitor;

7 Journalists (Robert and Alex Folger (*The Chronicle*), HJ Osbourne (*The Free Press*));

1 Notary Public;   2 U.S. Surveyors;

1 Court Commissioner (?);

1 Mining Engineer (Earnest Moss);

2 Dentists (23-year-old WP Jones and 29-year-old RG Pushaw);

1 Actor, Alfred Graham;

1 Assayer & Mining Expert, James Sperling;

5 generic "Agents";

1 Loan Office, T Eprain;   1 U. S. Postmaster, Geo. Putnam,

1 Register, JE Goodall;9 Musicians;

1 Stock Dealer; 1 Showman;

1 Gambler,   1 Secretary,

1 Business Manager.

Bodie 1880 Public Servants

James Grant, age 31, deputy sheriff;

William Atlee, age 55, Wells Fargo agent;

John Kirgan, age 52, single, Jailer; as well as, 1 Chinese cook in the jail;

3 Constables (Joseph Farnsworth ,age 36 and married, J S Harrington age 31, married as well, R Christian age 56, married, and John Roberts, age 37 and single);

Peter Taylor, age 37, married, Sheriff of the County;

RL Peterson, 30 years and married, Justice of the Peace;

2 "Com" Wardens, Irving Trowbridge and Allen Welton.

The one Minister listed is 52-year-old GB Hinkle, married, who preached at the still- standing Methodist Church of Bodie. Although the Owens Valley Catholic Priest, Father Cassien, was definitely a frequent visitor, the Catholic Church of St. John the Baptist would not be built completely for about two more years, and mass was said at the Miners Union Hall. He must have been on his rounds up and down the Owens Valley parishes, since he is not counted for Bodie.

Agriculturalists Included:

5 Milk Dairy(men), including Almond Huntoon;

3 Ranchers;

5 Farmers.

So what were the fair ladies of Bodie listed as doing to occupy their time?

One thing is certain—respectable females (approximately 454 listed) out-numbered the more famous maidens of Virgin Alley (only about twenty of these ladies are enumerated by name).

By far the largest group is categorized as "housewife," with a husband living in Bodie. There were 339 respectable ladies whose entire existence was in caring for house and children, cooking dinner, scrubbing, and mending by candlelight, far into the darkness of the Bodie night.

Photo courtesy of Mono County Historical Society . Helen Kernohan Sawyer's children—Robert, Nellie, and Lyna May Sawyer.

The youngest housewife was Maria Priday, age 16, married to Claud, a saloonkeeper.

The majority were much more mature-in their late twenties, thirties and early forties. The oldest wife was fifty-eight, and many were in their fifties. Most were immigrants from the East Coast and from Europe, with a sprinkling of Spanish-heritage Californians and Mexican natives. The housewives were predominantly Caucasian. I think I have mentioned the thirteen Chinese wives, which some say may have been prostitutes in reality—none have names and will thus remain hidden in the ashes.

An additional seventeen women were in that respectable, perhaps old-fashioned class, of relatives with no occupation, living with other family members in Bodie. Of these there were twelve "sisters" ages thirteen to forty years. Three women were unmarried "daughters" (ages nineteen to twenty-six), and two were mothers-in-law (ages fifty-one and seventy-five). The seventy-five-year-old Widow Mary Brown was the mother-in-law of Rev. Hinkle.

As opposed to the "relatives" category, there seems to have been another group of women with no perceivable occupation, yet whom I believe were considered "respectable." These consist of a group of married women who had children living with them—Bridget Sullivan, age fifty, and Mary Shewan, age fifty-two, Charlette Noble, age thirty-one, and Jane Hornbeck, age forty.

Emma Barnes, age thirty-f0ur, was listed as a divorced woman.

In the sad tradition of mining camps, there were several widows: Mary Cook, thirty-six; Mrs. Greer, forty; Sarah Johnson, thirty-eight; Mary Dunston, fifty; Ellen Sweeny, thirty-one; Eliza Hooper, forty; Kate Elliot, thirty; Martha McLeod, thirty-six; and Maria Kelton, forty-three. Many of these ladies had children living with them.

There was also a listing of some single women, whom I felt belonged in the respectable class: Hellen McQueen, twenty-three; Ella Blackmere, twenty-two; Maggie Constable, fourteen; Mary Gallager, forty; and Rose Summers, twenty-three. The placement of these women in the vicinity of several respectable family groups seemed to suggest that these ladies were part of some sort of extended family that was not explicitly mentioned in the census report. In the census report, there was a domicile number to indicate a building. That was in the first column, then the name of the head of the household, wife, children, and then, if there was another name without a new domicile number, it was a person living with that family—au pair, boarder, handyman, etc. who was not identified other than by name.

The other women living in Bodie were many of the new class of respectable "working women;" women who may be married but are listed as doing meaningful work outside the home.

Bodie window (photo by author)

The first were women doing services for the community that were very similar to occupations that were traditional duties many married women did inside their homes. The difference is that this group, through hardship or a desire to better themselves, took the home craft skills into the business level. By working outside the home these women raised the public tolerance for women branching out into the male-dominated work force. Respectable women could support themselves when they desired to do so, or when circumstances demanded it. Being a young and educated woman myself I felt sympathy for their courage to make a better life and a pride in our town.

I spent considerable hours reading and counting all the members of the 1880 Bodie Census and I freely acknowledge that, as a human being, counting and sorting through all these folks presented numerous challenges. All the mistakes were my own and I tried diligently to record all the working ladies of Bodie by name, age, married status and birth country or state. I am almost sure I missed at least one and apologize for any misrepresentation that my own lack of scholarship presented.

Nine enterprising women managed lodging houses: These ladies were Annie O'Neil, fifty, single, born in Ireland; Maria F. Fannon, thirty-four, widowed, born in Georgia, and raising three daughters ages sixteen, fourteen, and ten; Bridget McKinney, thirty-four, married to Edward, a native of Ireland; L.J. Bennett, thirty-nine, widowed, from Illinois; J.E. Harrison, thirty-seven, widowed, with two sons ages sixteen and twelve; Cramenta Johnson, fifty-three, widowed, native of Mississippi; Anna Swift, forty-seven, widowed, born in Kentucky; and Jennie Fisher, thirty-three, married, from New York.

Six ladies managed boardinghouses, meaning board, or meals, were provided as well as rooms. In the rough-and-tumble atmosphere of a high-altitude mining camp, these amazing women were able to transport their lodgers to a warm abode that welcomed them with the smells of a good kitchen. Their names are scant tribute to the real persons. Undoubtedly they worked many hours doing the cooking personally, and if no youngster was available, the cleaning of the whole place as well. Pennies only were probably made after expenses were paid out to the grocer and the woodcutter. But it was a foot forward, and better than the lot of others. There was Harritt Bowker, age forty, widowed, born in Michigan, whose son, age twenty-two, still resided with her, as did her daughter and her husband, who was himself a young miner. The family worked as a team to provide board to others who had livelihoods about the town or mines. There was a wide range in ages: Martha Dunlap, age sixty, single, immigrant from Wisconsin; Carrie Dunlap, age eighteen, single, born in Missouri; Martha Peterson, age thirty-two, single, all the way from Sweden; Mary McCarthy, age twenty-seven, single, born in Ireland. A look through the newspapers of that day usually show that the women paired up together to open these establishments, and probably each had their strengths. One partner perhaps did the cooking and the books, and the other the sprucing up and taking charge of the unavoidable laundry chores. One intrepid housekeeper, Kate Tobin, at twenty-nine and a native of Ireland, was married to a miner, and most probably opened her small miners' quarters to bring in a bit of cash to put aside for a rainy day. It was not easy work, but it created a spirit of financial security among these ladies and served as inspiration to their children and families.

One lady operated her own saloon: Maria Hall, age thirty-eight, single, born in New York. Owning such an establishment would place Maria outside of the respectable class, but for her to brave the all-male domain marks her as a strong woman. Her story is not known to me, but she is a testament to the ability of the female business sense that she was making a go of it. Three women operated their own restaurants. Such places were small, with home-type cooking, and had living quarters to the rear of the establishment.

In the wide-open days when Bodie's mines were supporting more than one shift each twenty-four-hour period, a smart cook was open for unusual hours to catch these miners coming off shift and looking for a bit of nourishment. Alcohol was never served in these establishments. That relaxation was reserved for the fine restaurants attached to the bigger hotels and the saloons of Main Street in Bodie. These were Martha Clark, age forty-eight, married with two children, born in Ireland; Annie Wiley, age forty-eight, widowed, born in New York; and one of the most well-known— Margaret Shaughnessy, age fifty, married, her miner husband gone off to the next excitement, all the way to Australia, born in Ireland and supporting four children and one grandchild. Her eldest daughter Katie was known to perform in respectable dramatic efforts about town. [Author's note: Katie eventually married Michael Cody, the land grant agent of Bodie and later one of the well-known sheriffs of Bridgeport. Katie and Michael raised four children in Bridgeport and Bodie, and their daughter Ella grew up to be a schoolteacher at the Bodie School, the writer of several historical books, and the wife of Victor Cain.]

MONO HOUSE
MILL STREET, ONE DOOR EAST
OF MAIN, BODIE
F. King & Lucy Bennett, Props.
This FINE HOTEL IS FURNISHED
IN ELEGANT STYLE

Throughout, and the accommodations
For guests cannot be surpassed.
THE ROOMS
Are large, airy and neatly furnished,
Provided with stoves and every conv-
enience known to a comfortable home,
Charges in accordance with the times.
Patronage solicited.
The Daily Free Press
August, 1880

HOTELS PRIVATE BOARDING
MRS. M. E. CHESTNUT
HAS LEASED THE
GRAND CENTRAL HOTEL
DINING ROOM AND ROOMS
BOARD—$9 per week
MEALS—50 cents
The Daily Free Press
Sept., 18, 1880

Home Comforts.
The most popular and best regulated restaurant in this town
is kept by Mrs. Chestnut. The place is patronized by all who
enjoy good meals and the quiet of a private house. Meals are
now cooked to order at all hours of the day and served in an
elegant style. Only the best cooks to be found are employed. This
restaurant is a few doors south of West & Bryant's store, on the
east side of Main Street.
The Daily Free Press
1880

STEWART'S HOTEL.
Lower Main Street
BODIE......CALIFORNIA
Mrs. Stewart, Proprietress
This Hotel has been entirely
Refitted, and is now in every respect
A First-class hotel, where patrons
receive courteous attention and all
The Comforts of a home,
is under the direct supervision of Mrs.
Stewart. The tables are supplied with
The best the market affords. Lady
Attendants give every possible attention
To Patrons. Patronage solicited.
Mrs. M. Y. Stewart
The Daily Free Press
January 1881

Two ladies earned a living as a cook: Kate Beaton, age twenty-three, single and born in Canada; and Anna Nelson, age thirty-five, married and born in Germany. A good cook had to always have a pleasant disposition to do well—the heat from the kitchen was wilting, the noise of the chattering pots and silverware could be very distracting, and the long hours were all spent rushing about.

Bodie had four waitresses as well: Annie Coen, age seventeen, single, born in Ireland; Nellie Devine, age nineteen, single, born in Ireland; and Mary Boyle, age twenty, single, also born in Ireland. Waitresses I always felt had to be very strong to carry the heavy porcelain plates piled high with biscuits, gravy, eggs, and meats–big meals to keep the big men working. I admired their starched aprons, always kept spotless, and thought their petite cotton headgear was very attractive.

Housekeepers and domestic servants were in high demand: Angelina, age twenty-four, married, born in Italy; Jane Brusse, age forty, married, born in Pennsylvania; Mary Watson, age fifty, married, born in Ireland; Mary Williams, age fifty-one, single, born in Ireland; Kitty Slade, age twenty-two, single, born in Bavaria; Flora Franks, age thirty, single, born in Prussia; Katie Carroll, age twenty-one, single, born in Canada; Addie Travers, age twenty-three, single, born in Massachusetts; and Lillie Lee, age twenty-eight, single, born in Ohio. A housekeeper was a woman of some experience beating the rugs and toting the hot water buckets for the family's laundry and bathing. She had to be sharp not to let the trades people overcharge her, as it would surely come out of her own expected salary. Mostly housekeepers ran a place where upper-class men were still single, or their wives were still back home and the men were too occupied to keep their own house in order, paying good money for these ladies to keep up the standards they wanted.

Many more were domestic servants and were listed with the household in which they were working (usually the mining superintendents'): Martina Gonzalez, twenty-five, married, of Mexico; Mary Patterson, twenty-eight, single, of Sweden; Lavinia Dougherty, twenty-one, single; Luvinia Barton, twelve, single; Belle Boyd, twenty-four, single, of Canada; Mary Ann O'Brien, twenty, single, of Ireland; Mary Gabion, forty-seven, single, of France; Louisa Showers, forty-five, married, of Michigan; Martha Botsford, forty, widowed with one son, of Michigan; Annie Cook, thirty-eight, single, of Ireland, Stella Howard, twenty-four, single, of California; Mary Conway, twenty-five, single, of Ireland; Martha Barrous, seventeen, single, of California; Addie Howard, twenty-four, single, of California, Mattie Jones, forty, widowed, of New York; Mary Dolan, twenty-six, single, of Ireland. I am sure these women counted themselves among the lucky—most, as you can see, had come a long way and their dreams could only be unfolding. Perhaps they hoped to be married and soon raise their own children, but they did honest work and Bodie welcomed them.

Rounding up the feminine services are three intrepid ladies in laundry enterprises. Competing in this Chinese-dominated market was not easy, but Annie Murphy, age forty, widowed, born in Ireland; Margaret Cargill, age forty-five, widowed, born in Ireland, and Margaret Travers, age twenty-nine, single, also born in Ireland, gave it a good run. Many folks appreciated looking their best, and a good laundress who knew how to iron, starch, mend a cuff, or replace a button was as valuable as gold.

MRS. O'NEIL'S BOARDING HOUSE
NEAR THE BODIE MINE
Having opened this place I will give
GOOD BOARD FOR $1 DOLLAR
PER DAY.
Or board and lodging
THIRTY-FIVE DOLLARS PER
MONTH.
Patronage solicited.
Mrs. O'NEIL
The Daily Free Press
Sept. 19, 1880

The California
Mrs. L. Keating and Miss Ryan have just opened the

California Boarding House on Mill Street. The ladies propose
to keep a good place and charge the moderate sum of $7 per
week.
The Daily Free Press 6-7-1880
Misses McCarthy & Kelly
Proprietors of the
GOLD HILL RESTAURANT
Opposite Miner's Union Hall
Respectfully announce
That they have raised the board to
$8 PER WEEK
The custom of the public is invited.
Bodie, October 18, 1880
The Daily Free Press
1880

THE CUFF HOUSE
(On The Hill)
Between the Standard and Bodie Mines
Mrs. Shaughnessy, Proprietress, wishes to
Inform the public that she has taken the above
House, and trusts, by strict attention to the
Requirements of the guests, to continue the
Patronage so liberally bestowed upon its late
Proprietor, Mr. Jacob Tautphaus.
Bodie, Cal, June 3, 1880
The Daily Free Press
June 3, 1880

SITUATION WANTED
By a young lady to wait on the table, do general house-work or

chamber work. Good references. Inquire at this office.
The Daily Free Press
June 6, 1880

BODIE HOUSE.
BOARD AND LODGING AT
TEN DOLLARS PER WEEK.
Wanted–Two neat Waiter Girls in the above house.
The Daily Free Press
August 1880

These three trades were occupied by women: dressmakers, milliners, and hairdressers. I so admired these highly-skilled ladies—dresses could always be hand- sewn by most women—my own aunt and mother had remarkable results. But a special dress, say for church or a wedding, made any woman desire the services of someone with a trained eye for the latest fashions from San Francisco and Virginia City. Having a talent and backed by experience, the tradeswomen could do very well if they also had business sense.

The women who lived in Bodie provided plenty of desire for pretty clothing, and Mary Ann Benton, age thirty-eight, widowed with one sixteen-year-old daughter, born in England; Mary Ann Lecord, age twenty-seven, single, born in California; Bertha Clements, age thirty-three, single, born in Germany; Carrie Goodban, married to Edward who owed a restaurant, with two daughters of five and three, born in the Utah Territories; Minnie Shafus, age twenty-five, widowed, born in Germany; Zeola Violette, age twenty-three, single, of Mexico; Carrie Munson, age nineteen, single, born in Connecticut, all delivered the dresses.

There were three milliners (hat-makers): Sarah Loryea, age forty-two, married, born in Poland; Caroline Dora, age thirty-two, single, born in Prussia; and Alice Howard, age twenty-two, single, born in California.

There were also two hairdressers: Jane E. Carter, an African-American, age thirty, single, born in Connecticut; and Agnes Carter, listed as mulatto, age twenty-four, single, born in California. These two ladies were perhaps related, but the census does not list them as such. Women of 1880 must all keep their tresses as long as possible and curled up about the face; most ladies did their own style. Some of our newer residents were accustomed to city life and the latest look was very desirable—Mother said it was good money wasted by a night's rest. I loved to look at the results, but truthfully never had spare cash for such luxuries.

There was also one butcher, a Joan Conslades, twenty-eight, single, born in Mexico. This seems to be a unique career choice, and perhaps there was an error in the census.

The two women of the professional class were, of course, of the most typical one open to educated women, schoolteachers at the Bodie School. These are Belle Donnally, age thirty-one, single, born in New York, who is credited as the first schoolteacher of the Bodie School District, but before that organization, I personally had many fine teachers. Joining Miss Donnally is Sarah Summers, age thirty, married, born in Mississippi. The Summers are longtime residents of Bridgeport and now Bodie, and the father and son are very qualified physicians for our area. Mother is acquainted with Sarah's mother, Mrs. Summers, and the younger sister Rose. Mother's eyes shined to think that education benefited such a deserving family, and Sarah always stopped in to give me a word of praise that I graduated from our Bodie schools.

There is also one lady who claimed to be a tourist, a gentlewoman by the name of Alma Curtain, single, twenty-nine years of age, and hailing from Kentucky. Her choice in labels always did bring a smile to our faces. In the old days, folks walked from

Kentucky to find new homes. Now folks traveled about, just for fun! I never met Miss Alma Curtain, but my eyes were opened just thinking that our Bodie was now a place folks would go out of their way to look over and learn how things were done in the new mining towns of the West.

> *RECEPTION. Mrs. C. Corbett and Miss Gill will give a reception at their millinery and dressmaking parlors, in the American House, up stairs, opposite the Occidental Hotel, on Saturday, November 8th, from 1-9 P.M., where there will be a full display of the latest styles of millinery and dressmaking, the ladies of Bodie are invited to call and see their goods.*
> *The Daily Free Press 1880*
> *MILLINERY.*
> *EMPORIUM OF FASHION!*
> *The Largest and Finest Stock of*
> *MILLINERY GOODS!*
> *Ever shown in Bodie can be seen at*
> *MME. DE VINE'S*
> *MILLINERY DEPARTMENT*
> *AT*
> *A.HAAS'S STORE, NEAR POST OFFICE*
> The Daily Free Press
> June 3, 1880

Window shot, Bodie, by the author

And lastly, one poor soul who is simply listed as "sick in hospital:" Eliza Pierce, thirty-six, single, born in Scotland. I always hoped Miss Pierce recuperated, and Mother said sure enough she would.

I was very proud to think what a fine town Bodie had become. Living there most of my life, I got to take a better look at it. I told Mother that western women and their ability to earn money outside the home is planting the seeds of change. My daughter would be raised in a civilized land that would send her to school and maybe even college. Mother would smile, remembering her life as a wife at the whim of her husband. If it was his dream to seek gold, the family would be transplanted across the gold fields of

California and the West. When the gold did not pan out, she took in laundry and baked pies (if she was virtuous), and made money her husband perhaps could not.

[Author's Note: Her daughter (1880s-1900s), married, might open up a small business of storekeeping, cooking, or a boardinghouse. But her granddaughter (1900s-1920s) was more likely to stay in school until she was eighteen or older, learning to read and write. New careers as accountants, bank clerks, postmistresses, nurses, and of course teacher, became available. The education of girls from the 1880s to 1900 eventually created a class of literate women. Literacy quietly changed the role of women for the rest of American history, setting an example for the rest of our world that is still quietly unfolding today.]

> *A MAN CANNOT POSSESS ANYTHING THAT IS*
> *BETTER THAN A GOOD WOMAN, NOR IS WORSE*
> *THAN A BAD ONE.*
>
> –The Bodie Chronicle
> August 11, 1880

Elizabeth Anne Butler, 1860s
Mono County Historical Photo

CHAPTER SEVEN:

LIFE IS LIKE A BLANKET

You can't have everything you want in this world. Life is like a blanket that is too short; if you pull it up over your shoulders you uncover your feet; if you cover your feet your shoulders must be bare. However, some manage to draw their feet up a little and pass a pleasant night.

The Bodie Chronicle
Dec. 12, 1878

My name is Elizabeth. I feel that my life has been caught in a dream that is so vivid that when I awaken I can still smell and feel it. In the dream, my mother is rocking me and I am a very small girl; my pigtails are being blown in the musty wind that brings the downpours that hit the dust on our farm so hard that you can see the little circles of dirt jump right up into the air. Suddenly, the rocking arms of my mother fade and it is now the rocking of the wagon, the big oxen grunting, and it is the smell of the prairie grasses, so strong that you almost choke with the scent of the animals and the dry wind and the heat just wilting you.

I am walking now. It seems like forever. I know my brothers, Ben and Will, would never leave me alone out here under this scorched blue sky, but all I sense is the giant wagon, the rocking, and the animal smells caught up with the sharp tang of the thirsty grasses. Suddenly, every time, I wake up and instead of the wagon I am surrounded with the sage brush and the rustling of the wind playing a clang-clang melody with the unlatched gate.

I am at home in my bed, it is just before dawn, and it is time to awaken the kitchen embers and get the morning meal for my husband, who gets up before dawn in freezing weather to tend to the dairy cows, or the haying, or the fence mending. Work on the dairy ranch is never ending.

My husband is a good man, plain to look upon, but then I am not a young girl either. I am strong-boned and made to work the day long, and yes, strong-willed as well.

I am past my fortieth year, but my hair is still dark and thick in its braid, and I stand up straight and know my way.

It is 1878, and though born in Wisconsin away across the land, I look out now through the wavy window of my kitchen, and already, the buzzing and the pounding of the mills that dot these high plains are telling me, girl, you are back in Bodie.

Mind you, Bodie has got in my blood. I have no yearning for the precious yellow metal that has ruined so many about me, but I don't begrudge them that mine the gold. That is their calling, and like me, they will answer at the end for how they dug their own ditch.

My first husband (I told you I was no girl) had that yearning fever so hard it about took his soul. He was a strong fellow, full of the passion of life, and my silly young girlish notions got the best of me when I thought I could settle him. Robert had the gold in his blood so strong that no girl could bleed it out to save him.

Believe me, I tried with all my heart to be a good wife and mother of his only girl child. When that man said move, in those first years, I packed up the baby, and the linens, and the bits of crockery that survived, and loaded the wagon myself, and drove it, too. I am not a fancy lady, but I am one to get the job done to the very end.

Robert Kernohan is his name still, although we are no longer married. You want to know, did I divorce the husband that God gave to me to love and obey until death do us part?

A pail of milk standing ten minutes where it's exposed to the scent of a strong smelling stable, or any other offensive odor, will imbibe a taint that will never leave it.

–THE BODIE CHRONICLE

DEC. 1878

Bodie (Photo by Author)

That is where that dream comes back. It's like that in real life. First your momma is rocking you, and then your brothers have done left you plumb in the middle of the prairie.

It is hard for me to say this, but Robert up and left. Hard times in Bodie camp came upon us after several lean years back in the late 1860s, but my brothers were still digging away, and just about to make good. Even so, Robert got wind of another excitement and he was determined to go off chasing another flash.

"Pack up the linens, wife, we are set for Washington Territories."

Something just didn't sound right about this move. Winter was coming on, and our little cabin at the Bodie camp had a new stove and a piece of wool carpet, with new curtains at the one window. Little Helen, our only daughter, had never seen a home that didn't get pulled right out from under her, and now it was time to think about organizing some kind of school for her to attend. Helen was already well past schooling age, and all Robert could talk about was moving again, farther away from home and family and schools, and settled womenfolk things such as a grocery store, where a lady could find a bit of ribbon to tack on her church dress, coffee was not just already-used grounds, and flour hadn't weevils in it.

It took all my courage to stand up to the husband I was sworn to love and obey, but I just had to think about my child. I pleaded: just wait until spring, maybe things will get better here, and the claims would begin to pay out something other than hard, back-breaking work—but I don't think Robert heard me at all, what with the buzz of a new golden dream spinning in his heart.

I came to realize that right now it was Washington, but a few years on, it would be Montana, and then some other territory. It wasn't the gold Robert sought, I got to thinking—it was the con-stant adventuring and the searching that had caught him up and consumed him. His wife and child just disappeared alongside those big thoughts. I tried my hardest to convince Robert to give up his quest, but all the time the voice inside me got stronger, and it was no surprise to me when Robert determined to go off alone.

Without Robert, I would have to rely on Wilson and Ben, my kin. I knew that they would always have a place for me—but there was a new voice in my head that said: "Wait up, girl! You've got more in you than a flower wilted after the first bloom of spring. You can work by doing what others can't do for themselves—you can cook, clean, and take in laundry and sewing!"

Robert sold off the cabin that was our home to get a stake, and my brothers cashed out a bit to buy him out of their joint claims. Wilson took his leaving quietly, never thinking Robert was the man to raise and stand by a family. Ben and his wife welcomed me into their home in Aurora, but that camp was declining rapidly, and besides, even the school was having trouble staying open. Decent work for a woman alone with a small girl was very hard to get.

I talked to most everyone of the local folk, and the best prospect seemed to be south a bit in the Bishop Creek Camp. I heard they had a good ranching community started, with womenfolk and children that were starting a school in the coming year.

I knew a kindly man who came by regularly to take advantage of my cooking. He told me of a lodging house in Bishop Creek that needed a woman to help out, and that a small lodging for Helen and me could be obtained. He said my cooking would secure any position I wanted to support me and my child without straying over into the moral shadows. So Helen and I set out for Bishop Creek.

My brothers were beset with their own difficulties—the Aurora diggings were going bust, and the Bodie camp was barely hanging on. Wilson had set up a blacksmith shop, and kept up a gold mining partnership with Ben and the last of the stragglers in the Bodie diggings. Ben had to have a sideline as well; he had two small boys to feed now and a city-bred wife. He was determined to support his family by cutting and selling wood, a valuable commodity in the cold winters and absolutely necessary for the steam engines of the gold-stamping mills.

We were all struggling to get a foothold, but we stuck together as a family. The brothers helped me move my household goods to Bishop Creek. I managed to get honest work cooking and cleaning a respectable lodging stop. Helen started school, and we could attend church services, so we could be proud that our family never let go of the values our folks had raised us to hold on to.

As years passed, I could scarcely remember Robert's face. There was no word from him or of him. Like so many men, he seemed to just step off into the wilderness and vanish.

Ben was always at me to move back to the Bodie camp, since finally the mines were attracting men and money from San Francisco, and machinery was being brought in to dig into the depths where gold was now real. Shops of all sorts were being opened, hotels were being built to accommodate the newcomers, and society was returning to please the first families returning to Bodie.

Wilson's blacksmithing had plenty of business, as wagons and freighting were beginning to be as valuable as the gold itself. Good times were coming; everybody talked of it.

Only a ring is necessary to engage a wife, but nothing short of cash will secure a good hired girl.
The Bodie Chronicle
September 25, 1880

Improvements.—Building in Bodie for the week past has been going on as rapidly as at any time this fall... We are glad to hear the click of the hammer, and the buzzing saw in Bodie from morn until night.
The Bodie Standard
Nov. 7, 1877

Pleasant Party-On Monday evening one of the most pleasant gatherings it has been our lot to attend took place at Brown's Hotel. Notwithstanding the storm of the two days proceeding had deterred many from coming from Bridgeport and Aurora, the hall was comfortably filled. Capt. Porter's quadrille band furnished good music. The hall was tastefully decorated, and dancing commenced at a seasonable hour, all entering into the spirit of the affair from the start... of the gentlemen present Mr. Butler...
The Bodie Standard Newspaper
Nov. 14, 1877

LETTER FROM BODIE
Too Many Men—Business Prospects
Correspondence Carson APPEAL
Bodie, Cal. Nov 15, 1877.
Editor APPEAL: According to promise I send you a short

> *communication from this thriving camp. I arrived today after a hard trip, and met with a most cordial reception. The town presents a very lively appearance, but you can assure your readers that there are more men here than can procure employment. They had better wait until spring, when there will be plenty of openings. The camp cannot be said to be over done, but it will be if there is any more crowding in. There are three general merchandising houses, of which Gilson & Barber of your city are the most prominent. A dozen or more saloons, six restaurants, one tin shop, one shoemaker shop, and other businesses are represented. The mines are all looking well and the camp has a bright future. Everybody is preparing for a hard winter; wood is high and hard to get...*
>
> M.B.
>
> The Bodie Standard Newspaper
>
> Nov. 21, 1877

I spoke of my sorrow and my doubts to my pastor in Bishop, and as a practical man he advised me to annul my banns with Robert. The Pastor was a man who understood that the West created its own rules, and he felt God never meant a good working woman to be wasted when there were plenty of men needing a wife's care.

So it was that this working girl was freed from her past, and soon opened up a new hope for me.

When I met Mr. Almond Huntoon, who made his living farming and raising dairy cows, I saw that there was a light shining bright in the morning after a long winter's darkness. Our courtship was as proper as any that Ma and Pa could hope for me after my long sorrow, and we planned to marry at the county seat in Bridgeport in a legal civil ceremony.

Almond Huntoon, 1870s
Mono County Historical Society Photo

My brothers were very happy at my good fortune; Mr. Huntoon and his brother Sidney were old-timers in the Bridgeport and Bodie areas, and were welcomed in all the respectable circles.

Mr. Huntoon had the dairy to rely upon, but his goal was to build a fine lodging house, ideally located on the new toll road proposed for travel to and from Bodie and Bridgeport.

New To-Day
A. HUNTOON
Will deliver
Fresh and Pure Milk
In and about Bodie
At Fifty Cents per Gallon
The Bodie Standard
May 15, 1878

THANKSGIVING BALL!
To be given at
McVarish & McLeod's New Building
(Corner King and Main Streets)
BODIE..............................CALIFORNIA.
ON
Thursday Evening, Nov. 29, 1877
(Thanksgiving Night)
Everything will be done by the proprietors to
Make this a most enjoyable affair for
All who may attend.
FLOOR DIRECTORS
F.B. HESSEL......................BODIE
B. F. BUTLER....................BODIE
F.G.DILLINGHAM...........AURORA
J.W.TOWIE...............BRIDGEPORT
JOHN CLUFF....................BODIE
C.W. MILLS......................BODIE
FLOOR MANAGER
SILAS B. SMITH
MUSIC BY PORTER'S STRING BAND

The public are respectfully invited to attend.
TICKETS $2.50

We are informed that the livery stable on Main Street, has been sold and that it will be remodeled and converted into a first-class hotel. Such improvement is very much needed in Bodie. There are no sleeping accommodations here commensurate with the demand, and daily increasing population.

Bodie continues as lively as ever. New faces appear on the street daily, and new buildings are seen in every direction. The entire available force in town and vicinity of mechanics, carpenters, and builders, are kept constantly employed, seven days a week, and cannot then begin to fill all the orders for new houses and business places...

–The Bodie Standard
Nov. 24, 1877

I felt his was a secure home for my now-almost-grown daughter Helen. At sixteen, school was still her proper place, and now with many womenfolk and children setting up in Bodie, I was sure that Bodie was going to be the home I had always dreamed of, with schools, grocery stores, and perhaps a church or two. As I looked back at my years in Bishop Creek, I thought fondly of those good folk that had given me their friendship and respect. All wished the best to me in that fall of 1877, and with many others I was returning to my Bodie with anticipation of better times ahead.

Mr. Huntoon took both my ability to work and my stubbornness with fairly equal sweetness. Bodie was fairly busting with good fortunes in 1877 and 1878. The mines were all reporting better each time the stockholders met. Tradesmen were flocking in, and all businesses were represented. What was lacking was housing—but where there is a will there is surely a way.

My brother Ben was turning board feet into a very comfortable living—so much easier than the old gold-digging days. His early real estate investments were turning into another fortune for him, and Ben was mentioned in all the local papers, from Bridgeport to Benton. He had associations with all the leading businessmen and time to invest in the new racetrack and be on the committees of the local events. His belief in Bodie was a testimony to sticking to this new place Mono County panned out with its gold.

Ben's example was quite an image for Mr. Huntoon and me. With my experience in hospitality trades, and with some shared convincing of Almond's brother Sidney, we were determined to borrow money from the Mono County Bank and build a hotel, right on the milk ranch property adjoining the Bridgeport road.

It was an exciting time for us. We engaged Ben to supply the wood and laborers, and Almond convinced a group of the old-timers—Mr. Day, Mr. Morris Dick, and some others—to invest with us in this sure-to-be-gold-mine.

Our place would supply all travelers' needs—stables, comfortable rooms, home cooking (that was me) and a well-stocked bar—a necessity in Bodie.

Will not some of the enterprising citizens of Bodie put up at once a good sized lodging house? Lumber can be obtained in any quantity at the saw mill at Adobe meadows. The roads are good and teams can make the trip there and back in eight days. Such an enterprise would be of great advantage to the town, and a good paying business from the start.

A petition is being signed by our citizens desiring the passage of an Act by the present legislature authorizing the supervisors of Mono County to set off that portion of Bridgeport township known as Bodie road district, into a new township, to be there after called Bodie township, and to have the same legal rights and privileges as other townships of the county now have.

The Bodie Standard

Dec. 5, 1877

BOOKER FLAT

HOTEL

ON THE BRIDGEPORT ROAD

Opposite the Noonday Mill

A. HUNTOON, Proprietor

This house has just been built and fixed
Up in good shape for patrons. All the com-
Forts of a country home will be found here,
And the table will be provided with the best
Of everything. A good bar is connected with the house, where
will be kept the best of
WINES, LIQUORS AND CIGARS.
Good accommodations for horses and stock.
The traveling public are respectfully invited to stop, and good
treatment is guaranteed.

Comstock Hotel
West side of Main Street, Bodie, California

A. HUNTOON, Proprietor
First-class Accommodations
For resident and transient guests. Comfortable beds and well-
lighted rooms.
Good Table Board
Always provided, and nothing will left undone to make
everybody comfortable.
The Bodie Free Press
July 17, 1880

But like I said before, just when you get comfortable on Ma's lap, you just might wake up on that wide-open prairie all alone and scared.

It seems like Mr. Huntoon had more heart than lodging house business sense. When times in Bodie were good, you could be surrounded by lots of folk looking to get a free ride on your claim. I guess I knew something was up, when the grocer would not let me have any more provisions on credit.

It wasn't just our bill that wasn't being paid—lots of good folks weren't paying us as mines closed down. Most of the paying mines even cut back to their most long-term crews, and these folks had wives to cook their meals and little wood houses of their own to go to, when the evening became chill. They did not have extra cash to come out to our beautiful place. And those that did mostly left before the dawn, not paying what was owed.

The high rollers moved on to the next excitement, and soon old friends were forced to visit Mr. Huntoon with faces of woe, followed by their lawyers. I sadly saw a big change in my husband when this came about.

I guess it was the old friends not sticking by that hurt the most, and Mr. Huntoon just seemed to cave in: "Elizabeth, my dear wife, I feel most of all for you! I promised to protect and support you, and, lord help me, I surely will, even if it kills me."

After all this, he went to his bed.

Of course, none of these financial setbacks mattered to me. I had been left high and dry before by so-called loved ones, and had picked myself up. I just didn't have the quit in me to let bad luck win out. I begged Almond to just get up and we could make another go. Ben was ready to help out, and other decent folks had lost their shirts in this Bodie bust. It wasn't any fault of Mr. Huntoon.

It seems like no matter how I prayed, pleaded, and cooked all his favorite things, Mr. Huntoon just decided already—his kind heart gave way, and bless him, he went-holding my hand and surrounded by his loving family.

Folks couldn't have been kinder to me, but work has always been my best medicine, and gathering family about me. I have the good fortune to be a hospitable, good-cooking type of lady, and those that will, always find a way.

Soon enough, I am mothering a whole passel of single miners, running the Syndicate Mine Lodging House, on the company payroll again.

I am wide awake right about now. I am not on the prairie. I am plumb right where my heart has always been—high up in the chaparral country of Bodie. The rolling of the wagon rocks me to sleep, and the bright light of another new day wakes me up.

Transfers of Real Estate.

Almond Huntoon to Mrs. E. A. Huntoon, land in Cotton-wood Canyon, love and affection.

The Chronicle Newspaper

Sept. 11, 1880

Sheriff's Sale

By virtue of an execution issued out of the Superior Court of the county of Mono, state of California, and to me, directed and delivered for a judgment rendered and entered in said Court on the 7th day of September, A.D. 1880, in favor of G. B. Day and against Almond Huntoon for the sum of $2,060.80 damages and $238.70 costs; and by virtue of another execution issued out of said Court and to me , directed and delivered, for a judgment rendered and entered in said Court on the 7th day of September,A.D.,1880 in favor of Morris Dick and against Almond Huntoon for the sum of$123.25 damages and 50.40 costs; and by virtue of another execution ordered by said Court and to me directed and delivered, for a judgment for a judgment rendered and delivered in said Court on said 7th day of September, A.D., 1880, in favor of James Sinnamon and against Almond Huntoon, for the sum of $528.87 damages and $60.90 costs:

I have levied on the following described real estate and all the right, title and interest of Almond Huntoon therein held by or standing in the name Sidney Huntoon, to wit... being the property known as the Huntoon Milk Ranch, and being the same tract of land on which Almond Huntoon has erected and now has a hotel known as the "Booker Flat Hotel"...

    Notice is hereby given that on the
    9ʰ Day of November, A. D. 1880

–The Chronicle Newspaper
October 16, 1880

Window shot, Bodie (Photo by Author)

CHAPTER EIGHT:

MEALS AT ALL HOURS

This is a wide world, and there is a place for everybody and everything in it.

In the long run men and institutions find their proper level. The good do not die young—or not always. They live to be useful and respected and their course marks the path of virtue and success.

The Daily Free Press
Monday, Nov. 3, 1879

Always try flour, butter, etc. before making a purchase, and you will save yourself much annoyance, as well as discomfort and mortification. You can never make good things of bad ingredients.

Mary Ann Mason, The Young Housewife's Counselor and
Friend, 1875.

My name is Jessie Delilah. I was born on January 6, 1883 in a four-room, two-story, wooden house on a dusty side street in this sagebrush land of gold. The place I was born is called Bodie, California and at 8,375 feet above the sea, proudly touching the sky. My hometown is constantly proclaiming the "difficulties" connected with living in this wind-swept alpine valley, a place of springtime rushing creeks, summer heat, and frigid winter snow piled into thirty-foot drifts—and a joke goes that this is just the weather for this week. Up a bit from my house, still on Green Street, the two-story board and batten school house stands, with a map of these United States proudly displaying something we all know—the town of Bodie is a mere speck in the grand span of the land, perched on the shoulders of the snowy Sierra Nevada mountain range, the blue waters of Mono Lake shimmering in the views one can see from the Bodie Bluffs, and the desolate deserts of the Nevada State border with California just about sucking dry any passing clouds of moisture. The map on the wall of my school does not do justice to the magnificent scenery of Bodie. Bodie's thin alpine air catches you trying to breathe in the vastness of the tumbling mountains that seem to fade as far away as the eye can see. The violet sky and the dry smell of sage is forever stamping the landscape of this place into your brain—dancing like memories of all the good times in a faded childhood scrapbook. The wooden buildings of Park Street and Main Street have turned silent, the paint has peeled off the fine homes, and dull flowered wallpaper flaps in the hot winds of summer. Broken bits of pottery, rusty square nails, and broken bottles are strewn across the old town site like an impressionistic mosaic of days gone by. Glass windows stare like eyes into the dark sky.

I can hear the voices of the town, even after all these years have melted away.

A dog barks a greeting to his master. Children's cries of discovery and play echo off the barren landscape. Mama's quiet voice murmurs inside the doorway of our home, and Papa's boots crunch the walkway after a long day at work. My brothers run, play "catch me if you can," yelp and tease. And always the dull pound of the great stamp mill, piercing the dawn and dusk, grinding out the glittering gold from the dark, deep earth. Adults laugh amid the evening chatter of dinner plates and glasses clinking. All the sounds we treasure in our hearts and hope to preserve for our babies, the sounds of home. Look into the windows of our town, into your own reflection, and you can still see us. We are your past; eating a quiet meal at the end of the day, glad to be surrounded by our loved ones. Come with me. I want to tell you my story. It is the real tale of Bodie, the most famous town of the golden days.

Jessie Delilah Cain-Mono County Historical Society

Historical Introduction

Frank S. Wedertz, in *Bodie. 1859-1900*, writes: A Mormon settler named Colt located the first quartz ledge claim on Copper Mountain, northwest of Mono Lake in 1854. Dogtown Creek (west of Bodie) was being panned with some luck by 1857, and such was the habit of the times, many more prospectors pushed down from Placerville, and Sonora. The Mono Diggings hit color in 1859. Some say they were on a reputed wild drinking binge which started on the Fourth of July.

The founding of the ensuing town of Monoville was actually credited to Cord Norst. It was located just over the hills from Bodie.

William Bodey blew into Dogtown from Tuolumne County amidst all the excitement. On a camping excursion with a few close buddies, he discovered placer gold somewhere in Taylor Canyon. It was the first gold discovered in the Bodie Hills.

After Bodey's demise in a November snowstorm in, 1859, activity at his gold discovery site followed the pattern familiar across California. The original placer gold was picked out of the streambeds by single miners standing in the icy waters, bent over panning out the heavier gold nuggets from the lighter sand and water.

Then the lone gold panner was replaced by a crew of men working together with simple mining machines like the "rocker," an oblong box without a top, several feet in length, mounted on a rocker and placed on a sloping surface. Dirt was shoveled n and buckets of water followed. As the miner rocked this cradle-like device, gold became trapped in ridges carved on the floor of the rocker.

Now the pan and cradle are replaced by quartz miners. Digging into the earth required capital and labor. Miners first joined together in formal and informal unions in the chase to "See the Elephant." When the first gold was found in 1849, it was two thousand miles from established law and order. Miners established their own rules, voluntarily organizing mining districts. Each district was named, and had an elected recorder of claims, and held firmly to its authority to settle disputes. A record was kept of each claim, the various districts adopting codes to fit the particular locale. The maximum size for each claim, the process to file claims, the manner of working the claim and the agreed-upon way claims were abandoned was written down.

Each district was operated in a democratic manner, but it was a closed society. Blacks, Asians and in many cases, Mexican and Latinos were excluded. District rules were often used to administer justice, banishing thieves and other wrongdoers. On occasion, continued abuse of the district "law" would result in a lynching.

As the gold in and around streambeds became exhausted, the so-called hard rock miners took over. Now men were digging shafts up to forty feet deep, horizontal tunnels—drifts—spider out into solid rock to locate the elusive veins of gold-bearing quartz.

The rumors of rich gold in the Bodie Hills struggled for almost fifteen years after William Bodey froze to death at the side of the road as if waiting for the invention in technology of deep gold mining caught up to organized financial capital investments structures which needed to be in place to pay for such an overwhelming endeavor.

By 1875, the town on the site of Bodey's original strike had achieved all the necessary components it needed: skilled men to mine the depths, capital backing from San Francisco and the East Coast, the outlines of a town, plenty of beer and whiskey, several dirt roads to other gold mining areas and a more poetic name. A sign painter liked the look of "Bodie" over the stable yard (instead of Bodey) and history discovered the newest darling in the civilizing of the West.

My papa, James Stuart Cain, was born on a farm just outside Rockburn, Canada, across from Chateauguay, New York. Born on April 17, 1853, Papa was the fourth child of Jennet Stuart and David Cain. His sisters were Bunny, Mary, Elizabeth, and Mina, and his brother was Isaac.

Grandpa David's family was second generation immigrants from Derry, Ireland. Life was not easy, and Grandpa struggled to feed his growing family. Far from green Ireland, Grandpa carved out a new life in this cold Canadian land. There was a call for sweets in this new place, and the maple trees in the frigid temperatures of the northern winters could provide a living for those who could turn the tree sap into gold. For maple sugar farmers, cold weather was a sign of good times and so for my Papa, cold weather has always been a good luck charm.

People love to complain about the Bodie weather with its twenty-foot snow drifts, wind, fog, and long winters. Papa always said: "Cold weather, you say? This is nothing to back home, where the colder weather brings a good crop of syrup and a better living to those who can farm it!"

When Papa was a young man, he just couldn't stay home with his parents anymore. James Stuart Cain got it into his head to come to the American West. The farm in Rockburn just wasn't exciting enough, what with everybody just buzzing about the golden hills of California where any man could easily make a fortune. A man could work a whole year and do well to make 300 dollars. Why, in California folks could pick that up in a month. With talk like this, it was no wonder a young man like Papa would want to do bigger things than farm maple trees.

My papa was able to do almost anything he put his heart into— James Stuart was tall, and quick to pick up on the detail of any trade as easy as looking at it, and could tell you a good joke while he was working. Getting along with other folk and working hard, Papa was due to be a success. He and his childhood friend Lester Bell made up to go West, and together they made their way. The transcontinental railroad was already built, and California was threaded with stage lines to every destination—so all Papa and Lester had to do was wave good-bye to family and friends, and from then on, the two stayed together on their wild adventures in golden California.

In 1877, the most popular end destination was the Comstock excitement, so Papa and Lester arrived in Carson City, Nevada young, strong, and willing.

The mines of the Comstock burrowed into the earth to retrieve gold so very deep that the most popular method of gold extraction was the so-called beehive style. The mine was formed up with timber to make a square block formation that shored up the digging a block at a time. Each cell of timber was formed up as the miners dug deeper, and the block constructions were much stronger when each square was separately formed. It was an engineering marvel that many folks said looked just like the cells that formed up a beehive.

James Stuart Cain in Carson City, 1870s
Mono County Historical Society Photo

If a fellow didn't have deep mining experiences, which of course Papa did not, the next best way to make a living was to look for work in the timber business. As mines were prospected, and the need for shoring timber grew, an enterprising fellow could make a business of locating trees. Those that were just right did not always grow where the gold was being mined, so after locating the best trees they must be cut down and dragged undamaged by mule teams to the sawmill. Only a few mills had the machinery for carving the wood into the form to be used to shore up the beehive of mines. Timber did not stop at the sawmill. Teamsters with enormous wagons and strong horses must transport the finished wood to the mines which, because most mines did not have main roads nearby, required another gang to clear and maintain a road. The weather could and did wipe out these roads every so often. Lastly, when the timbers made it to the mines, the

Historical and Geological Background

On January 24, 1849, James Marshall discovered placer gold at Sutter's Fort. Word spread around the world and all nationalities made their way to the newly-liberated California Territory. Perhaps as many as 80,000 gold seekers, mostly male, young, and single came to California in the first year after Marshall's discovery. Gold changed the economic fabric of the United States, and indeed the world. The search for gold became the extreme example of the new economic democracy. Any person willing to take the risk had a chance to become wealthy. California achieved statehood in 1850, mostly based on the acknowledged wealth this new land could bring to the union.

In the rest of the states, a young man could reasonably expect to earn a dollar a day as a farm laborer, and as much as $1.50 for skilled labor. Gold panning in California could average sixteen dollars a day washing gravel from the many streambeds. For the men and women traveling to California, the search for gold would become the significant adventure of their lives, one that was repeated for generations in stories. Historians estimate that less than one in twenty California gold seekers returned a profit for their grand adventure (www. californiahistory.net/text).

But many did return home to build greater fortunes with the golden profits. For example, Levi Strauss built an empire selling his famous pants. Collis P. Huntington started as a hardware merchant in Placerville and ended up as one of the Big Four who owned the railroads in the West. John Studebaker began by selling wheelbarrows to the miners and finished his life becoming a household name in automobiles, and Philip Danfort-Armour began cutting meat in Placerville and took his fortune back to Chicago, running one of the largest meatpacking businesses in the world.

The first arriving miners to reach California were amateurs. As the technology to profit from the gold boom increased in complexity, so too were the original immigrants replaced by men skilled in deep rock mining, displacing the first settlers into service- oriented occupations, where they became wealthy supporting the operation of the mines. Much has been written about the amazing gold riches that made the town of Bodie so romantic. Viewed in the clearer light of modern writers with a background in geology, the picture comes into focus. Michael H. Piatt presents a concise scientific offering in *The Technology of Mining Gold: Introduction to Bodie's Geology,* which helps shed a great deal of light on this difficult subject. According to Piatt's research, Bodie's gold bullion was made up of one-hundred-pound bars, which contained seventy-three pounds of silver and only twenty-seven pounds of gold, with the high silver content causing Bodie's bullion to be very pale. The meaning of "quartz mining" was broader in the 1880s, and quartz was defined as "any hard gold or silver, as distinguished from gravel or earth (Rossiter Raymond, *A Glossary of Mining and Metallurgical Terms,* 1881). Gold bullion is rarely pure, containing silver, lead, iron, copper, and sulfur in the Bodie mines. This dilution of the gold would determine the actual value of the various bars being shipped—ranging from the best, at about twelve dollars per ounce, to the least, about three dollars per ounce.

next step required great hordes of men to build the lumber into the structures needed inside the mines. As you can see, the timbering enterprise had plenty of room for a man like my papa.

Papa and Lester started out at the bottom of the timber business. They found jobs tending the flumes that were moving the logs cut in the area of Glenbrook, near to Lake Tahoe toward the great mining area of Virginia City. The flumes brought logs to Washoe Valley and Carson City, where they were cut into timbers and sent up to the mines. Tending the water-driven flumes could be dangerous work. If the great big logs decided to get stuck, the tender was the poor fellow who had to get it unstuck. With plenty of logs roaring down behind it, this could be the undoing of many a hopeful young man.

Papa always had the confidence to know that a man who saved his money could make his way faster than those fellows hanging about the saloons wasting it, and he saw that there was more money and security in the transportation and freighting business. Cut into timbers in the valleys, the wood needed to be hauled up to the mines. An enterprising fellow could take hold of a good business if he but dared. Papa got himself a set of mules and a deal on a transport wagon, and he was in business for himself. Soon he was successfully moving the timber beams to the V&T Railroad, which carried them up to the Comstock, showed off Papa's abilities, as well as his honesty and skill with numbers. Before long Papa got another promotion as foreman of the V&T Railroad, which didn't mean he got out of the mule team business—he just added a job to match his talents and saved more money.

Papa also met the men with power and money in this new land— that is, the railroaders. Men like these took the map of the frontier and made or broke big and little communities alike. Papa showed, with his hard work and his ability to get other men to get moving, that he was a fellow to be trusted. Men with money and power just depended on other folk, and James Stuart Cain became their man.

So now my papa, come down from Canada in 1874 at age twenty-one, able to read and write and work hard, was now, at the vigorous age of twenty-five, ready to hit the really big time.

The excitement everybody was now talking up is the rich diggings at Bodie, California. The mines were fabulously successful and investors were profiting a dollar a share- big money for the times. Optimistic talk burned like pine cones—fast and furious.

The newly organized *Bodie Free Press* was singing out the praises of the Bodie mines.

Perhaps without being aware of it himself, Papa was just about to really get on his way, and in his way stood Mama, the beautiful and strong-willed Martha Delilah Wells.

Mama's family had been real frontier Westerners, every generation born in another more westerly state or territory, marching their way across America seeking out opportunity and making a better home for the growing family.

Martha Delilah was born on June 3, 1861in Mormon Station (later renamed Genoa), the first permanent settlement in Western Utah Territory. Mama was born shortly after it had become the Territory of Nevada. Genoa was established in 1849 as a trading post for travelers heading for California. Mama and her older brother Jonathon and little sister Charity grew up moving to various desolate places of the Utah Territories, as her Papa tried all sorts of ventures to make a go of it.

The Wells family never did have it easy. Mama was not much of one to talk of bad times, but I pieced together slips of things she said. By the time my older brother Victor came along in June of 1880, Mama had lost both her mother, Victoria Gould, to an early death, and her own papa to that wanderlust that has taken so many western men. Grandpa Nathanial Wells ended up in the Montana Territories in the wood trade and mostly stayed gone for the rest of Mama's life, sending an occasional windfall back to Carson for Mrs. Gould, Mama's maternal grandma, who had taken in Mama and little Cherrie. Jonathon Wells, at their mother's death, was passed to the Wells relatives back over in Salt Lake. I knew those relatives to be Mormon, but I could never figure out if Mama was—her paternal uncle Heber Wells did well for himself later as a governor of Utah in the 1890s, and most of Utah's politicians in that day were Mormons.

Mama and her brother did correspond some, and no love is ever stronger than between kin who get separated by tragedy, but it was her little sister Cherrie that lived close to us after she grew up. Auntie Cherrie married Lester Bell, Papa's childhood friend, though of course this was some years coming about. The long and the short of it is that the Cains and the Bells were close, and settled down in Bodie for good.

Grandmama Abby Gould was a widow herself when she took on the two sisters, and though she was not to remarry, she had a clear view of what was proper and what was not. Mrs. Gould never let the wild places stand in the way of a proper upbringing. Mama was taught to mind and stay ladylike no matter the circumstances. I believe Mrs. Gould ran a boarding house in Carson City, but I was very young when she passed away and I do not recall much of this brave lady.

Mama herself never was too afraid of much that I ever saw, except that we children would have dirty faces or torn clothes when company unexpectedly showed up on our doorstep, which on account of Papa being very social happened quite a bit.

I don't really know how it was that Papa first saw Mama, but she was his beloved "Lile" until she died, and that was that. I know mama's kin were living near Carson City at this time, and Cherrie was about ten or eleven and still in school, when Papa decided to marry Mama. The wedding took place in Carson City on September 19, 1879.

Mama's beautiful eighteen-year-old face gazes at the wide world from her wedding photograph. Dressed in beautiful hand-sewn lace, she had stylish, gleaming pearls decorating her dark brown hair, which curled down over her shoulders in ringlets.

Papa looks fine beside her and so young. I always believed they were sitting because when standing, he towered above her petite frame. Papa always was broad in shoulder, with blond-brown hair and mustache. He looked wonderful dressed in a fine suit of clothing bought over in San Francisco. For me, the photograph of this couple is the very portrait of two young, brave adventurers.

Bodie was the place to go for any bright young man, so Papa made up his mind he would throw in with this exodus, and Mama was sure not going to be left behind. Mama had a sad time leaving her kin, especially Cherrie. Papa was ready to go on ahead and set up house in a rush to get on with his freighting business, but Mama didn't think highly of that. Papa wanted to travel light, but Mama decided to set up her house with all the items a proper lady had to have. Papa never could say no to his brown-haired sweetheart, Delilah. Papa might be a leader with businessmen, making plans of where to live, but Mama surely ruled at home.

In the brewing winter of 1879, Bodie was not a cheap camp with lots of dwellings available for families. There were no trees to speak of, so wood houses were definitely at a premium. Papa did his wife fine, and bought a nice two-story home right on the corner of Fuller and Green Streets, away from the rough life on eastern Main Street. The house had been built recently, but the previous family had had to move all of a sudden, so it was perfect for a family—built of wood and whitewashed at least once already, it sat on a partial stone raised foundation, with a small porch facing Green Street and those famous violet sunsets over the Sierra.

The best and warmest room was the large kitchen, located at the back, with a stove already assembled, and a sink with a drain that poured right outside. Mama did not have pump water in the first days, as the Bodie water system was still to be argued out. Mama had two choices: rely on the big horse-drawn water delivery wagon with its long wooden tank, paying a fee that sometimes stretched the weekly budget, or carry the water from the public well, which was not more than a street over. Folks just starting in Bodie got a chance to meet their neighbors at the well, but it is hard work, especially in bad weather. Either way, Mama was lucky to be setting up her own household. She also was proud of the cabinets already attached to the walls, in which to store her kitchen utensils. Best of all, the room had a small window that looked to the south and brought in friendly light. Right next to the kitchen was a dining room for everyday meals.

Near the south side of the yard we had a private privy set back about ten or so feet from the back of the kitchen (you surely don't fancy a long walk in winter cold, but you definitely want some distance in the heat of summer). At this time, there wasn't any plumbing set up for indoor toilet needs, and folks made do with the many outhouses that dotted the town, with most of the families having their own personal outhouse.

Mama's new house had a tall, carved, wooden door with a transom window over it to let in more light during the short days of winter, opening to air in the long, hot days of summer. Right inside was a charming parlor, favored with three very large glass windows—one to the north and two to the east to allow the welcome morning sunshine. Opposite the main door was also a fine curved staircase with a real banister of polished wood, leading upstairs to the two bedrooms. Flowered wallpaper lined the entry and stairs. The rooms upstairs were small, and the bed and other furniture took up most of the space, but the rooms were cozy and warm in winter, and the privacy of being away from downstairs was a precious commodity for me, living with three noisy brothers.

All in all, it was a home that any family in 1879 Bodie would love to occupy. My papa brought his wife to this home on the quiet side streets of Bodie. His Delilah never did live in a boardinghouse, like so many of the other women in town. The house was meant for us to put down roots, with the gold mines on the bluffs above the town and the wild life on Main Street just a murmur in the background of our life together.

This house changed quite a bit as our life in Bodie transformed—Mama and Papa raised all four of us children, three of us born right here in this very house. And we thought they did a mighty fine job of it.

Good times added new rooms, lean-tos, and comfort areas for those famous long, cold Bodie winters. A long, shaded porch was added later, and many an after-Sunday- dinner found our family and friends gathered here until the moon rose over the lavender hills.

This house on Green Street had an air of happy times, not fancy but warm. We children had a fenced yard where Mama could see us play, and a little gate led to the wide-open hills of Bodie. But Mama was one who always seemed to know all our secrets. Mostly she let us have them, as long as we didn't embarrass her or Papa in front of other folk.

Papa's business deals kept him busy almost all of the years we lived in Bodie. Papa is what folks called an entrepreneur—he worked at several ventures all at once and seemed to keep it all sorted out, keeping the goodwill of any who did business with him.

> *Accustom your daughters, while growing up, to aid you in culinary matters. Take care, before they marry, that they know how to perform all the duties of a housewife. Otherwise they may be unhappy, unprofitable wives, and more of a burden than a pleasure and comfort to their husbands. Do not fancy it unrefined for young ladies to enter the culinary domain. **No duty is unrefined.***
>
> *–Mary Ann Mason, The Young Wife's Counselor and Friend, 1875*

Sketch by the author of the Cain Family House,
Fuller and Green Streets, Bodie

> *"…A good housekeeper requires: tables, shelves, closets, pasteboards, sieves, tubs, pails, rolling-pins, trays, pots, pans, colanders, strainers, skimmers, a saw, hatchet, cleaver, scissors, mallet, sausage-grinder and stuffer, coffee-toaster, coffee-mill, tea-kettles, pots, mortar and pestle, soup, candles, ovens, or a first rate stove or range, tin baking-pans, furnaces, bell-metal kettles, porcelain kettles and stew pans, towels, boiling cloths, bread-towels, dish-cloths, salt, pepper, spices, etc., spice mills, egg-beaters, strainers, ladles and flesh-fork, bread-toasters, knives and forks, spoons, skewers, aprons, a kitchen clock. All these items are indispensable … to a fully-arranged kitchen…"*
> —Mary Ann Mason, *The Young Housewife's Counselor and Friend,* 1875

Papa's original colleague was Mr. Porter, who had established a lumber business in the first seasons of wide-open Bodie, 1878 to 1880. Mr. Porter became very successful, his business always doing its best to supply the lumber needs of the growing community and the timber-starved mines. Papa was the fellow who got the wood *to* Bodie. Papa could send out several large freight wagons, say over to the Bridgeport sawmills. He knew how much load each drover's wagon could handle, supplied the livestock and their feed, paid the tolls upfront, and paid off the men in cash upon delivery. His men handled twenty mule strings like they were babies, and drove across roads that were dusty, narrow, and steep in dry weather and washed out and rock- strewn in wet. In winter, they replaced the over-sized, wood-spoked, metal-rimmed wheels with runners and hauled their precious cargo on a sleigh in times people feared to go outdoors for any but the most vital of reasons. The forests were thirteen miles across the Big Meadow and the sawmills were further on, up Buckeye Canyon and Robinson Creek.

It was a golden opportunity to be in the business to supply the great hungry steam engines that stamped out the quartz, which was picked out with hand tools and manually shoveled into metal rail carts, which trusty mules pulled out of the deep holes in Bodie Bluff, as the Stamp Mills shook the town day and night.

When the Bridgeport Mills raised prices, Papa turned to other sources, always needing a constant supply of logs to supply his contract to Mr. Porter. The land on the far side of the great dead sea of Mono had been blessed with fine stands of virgin pine, tall and straight and plentiful. First, Papa turned his eyes toward the east and dealt with the two Vining brothers, using barges on the lake to shorten some of the treacherous land routes. But the lake is a mysterious and vengeful lady, and her deceptive blue waters could switch like a jealous lover to dark-wind driven chop, which turned more than one barge back to shore.

Folks who planned to stay, as well as the big mines, must have shelter and firewood from the awesome winters of the eight-thousand-foot Sierras. Papa had his own "wood" gold mine, and he made his way surely and steadily, working very hard for his new family.

Papa was always the center of our universe. Mama thought there could be no one brighter or more pleasing to look upon. And of course, my brother David Victor, me, known as "Doll," and little brothers Stuart and Jimmie, all agreed with Mama on most things, and especially on Papa.

Mama and Papa came to Bodie in the first bright light of their life together, and I think that is partly why we always cherished this place. Bodie was a brilliant star in the golden lands of California. The miners sweated to dig the gold, the mill-men stamped the gold, the fabricators melted the gold into heavy bars, the stagemen and their protectors transported the gold, and every man raised a toast as loud and constant as the eternal thumping of the gold mines. Optimism was the fuel of every hearth. Wintry blasts might rage outside, but mere weather could never daunt the people of Bodie.

The great cry in Bodie just now is wood! Everybody is asking his neighbor, "what are we going to do for wood?" Teams are hauling in as fast as possible, and still there is a limited supply for our rapidly increasing population. He price per cord has advanced during the last ten days to $14 per cord.

Thanksgiving was observed in Bodie—those who could not get turkey were satisfied with roast beef or baked beans.

Our mining companies are receiving large consignments of lumber and timber from Bridgeport, preparing for the winter.

G.L.PORTER & Co,
ARCHITECTS and BUILDERS
Estimates and Bills of Lumber made out. Also
Plans and specifications furnished on reasonable terms.
All kinds of jobbing and shop work done with neatness
And dispatch.
FURNITURE, DOORS, AND WINDOWS
MADE TO ORDER
COFFINS A SPECIALTY
Lots and buildings in the best part of the city for sale.
Long experience in the business and employing only first-class
mechanics; warrants us in guaranteeing satisfaction.
SHOP-CENTER MAIN STREET
BODIE MONO CO.   *California*

The Bodie Standard
November, 1878

Correspondence.

Mormon Station, December 20, 1878.
Thinking that a brief communication from this busy station on the Bodie road might be of interest to your readers, I will send you

a few facts… There passes here daily about 60,000 feet of lumber; about fifteen loads of freight; twelve to fifteen loads of fruit and vegetables; and , in addition to all this quite a number of teams pass daily here , loaded with chickens, turkeys, geese, ducks and pigs; and, additional, we see teams loaded with all kinds of household furniture, useful and worthless—all on the way to Bodie…

–The Bodie Chronicle
December 21, 1878

Doll, Vic, Stuart, and Jimmie Cain
Mono County Historical Society Photo

Rooms of eleven feet by thirty feet reached rents as high as one hundred dollars a month on Main Street that first winter of 1879.

The "supposed" bones of William S. Bodey lay in state, covered by a black cloth at the center of the Masonic Lodge. His ten-year resting place on the side of the Bridgeport road was gleefully resurrected by a group of leading citizens. William's whitened bones were to be re-interred amid great pomp, and a fitting ceremony for the founding father of Bodie.

Cuban cigars and beer from San Francisco could be bought downstairs at a decent establishment, while transient dentists operated in hotel rooms upstairs. Suits could be made in the latest fashion by a city tailor, and right next door there were barbers who could shave and fashion your hair. Public baths, silk underwear, sandwiches of all kinds, wines, liquors, saloons, furniture, bedding, miner's boots, fancy goods, dressed lumber, crockery—all could be had just a walk from our doorstep.

Bodie in 1879 was flush with good times, with gold bullion pouring into every pocket and all the services that gold could buy. High times brought jobs to the skilled and opportunities to those who took the risk.

My Papa, James Cain, and my Mama, Delilah Cain, are two of the folk who took that chance and survived every adversity that Bodie threw at them—the two stood side-by-side, strong through their lifetime of devotion to each other; a bond too strong for any gold town to break apart.

Bodie Timeline Important Dates in California History

Time Before the white explorers:

The Northern Paiute, locally called the Ku-ze-di-ka live in seasonal camps between Big Meadows (Bridgeport) in the summers and south to Hot Creek/Pinion

Pines areas about Benton in the winter. Master hunters, gathers of many local plants and insects, the Paiute are democratically organized, selecting leaders. Winnemucca was the last great chief of the entire Ute nation, and locally Captain Bob and then his son, John, led his tribe, until the 1918 world war broke up the tribes' local loyalties.

1828: Peter Ogden discovers the Humboldt River.

1833: Joseph Walker leads a group from the Green River to California and back, creating the California Trail.

1841: The Bidwell Party takes the first band of emigrants to California, making it as far as Nevada, with the first white woman and child.

1843: The Stevens Party are first to take wagons across the Sierra.

1844: Sarah Winnemucca is born; her uncle, Chief Truckee, helped General Fremont in the California war of liberation from Mexico. Sarah, as a young girl, lives with a white family, the Ormsbys, at Mormon Station (later renamed Genoa), a town near the 1861 birthplace of Martha Delilah Wells.

1848: Gold is discovered at Sutter's Mill.

1849: Twenty-five thousand people take the overland trail to the California gold fields.

1850: California, rich with gold, achieves statehood. Of the 57,787 immigrants who arrived in California five hundred are Chinese.

1850s: This decade sees a tremendous surge toward excess in the dress of women and children. Skirts widened, supported by flounces, laces, ribbons, and trimmings. Sara Josepha Hale of *Godey's Lady's Book* calls for simplicity in children's dress, saying "they are not puppets." Western women's dress is far more utilitarian when isolated in the small ranches, mining camps, and farms.

1851: U.S. Mail is carried by mules from Sacramento and Salt Lake.

1852: Of the 11,798 Chinese living in California, only seven are women.

1854: James Stuart Cain is born on April 17 in Canada.

1856: The first wagon road is built over the Sierra Nevada in August and runs from Murphy's Camp to Carson Valley, Nevada.

1859: William Bodey and his friends camp at the crossroads of the Sonora road, and William picks up placer gold in Taylor Canyon. Mr. Bodey cannot seem to wait for good weather and sets out for his lean-to cabin in November and perishes, survived only by his companion Black Taylor, a half breed. Taylor is later mysteriously hunted by the apparently-peaceful Paiutes, his body beheaded and scattered in the sagebrush of Benton.

1861: The Pony Express shortens the mail delivery.

~Bodie is not an organized town, but more of a camp, with about fifty residents living in various wood or adobe structures, with one boardinghouse, all up on the bluffs by the mines. There are no stores or restaurants, and supplies have to be obtained by traveling to Monoville or Aurora

~Mono County is created on April 24th; it is 150 miles in length and fifty miles wide, with Aurora as its county seat.

~A brick schoolhouse is constructed in Aurora for some eighty children.

~The Bunker Hill Mine on the Eastern Bodie Bluff is located on July 1. This name was later changed to The Standard. It is one of the richest eventual mines in the history of Bodie and the largest employer for most of Bodie's mining days.

~Martha Delilah Wells is born on June 3 in Genoa, Nevada Territory.

~Elizabeth Butler, who came to California by oxcart from Wisconsin with her many brothers, is married to Robert Kernohan.

1863:~Elizabeth Kernohan and her daughter Helen Anne take up residence in Bodie, the first white woman and child to do so, in a cabin on Browne Street

1868: The Central Pacific Railroad finally crosses Nevada.

CHAPTER NINE:
THREE KINDS OF TIME

"The Waste Dump"

Stage travel has been rather light the past few days.
Work on the water works reservoir is proceeding rapidly.
The Miners' Union will give a grand ball on Thanksgiving Eve.
Not to possess a cold or sore throat is to be out of fashion.

Bodie has three kinds of time at present—fast, slow and good times.

This snow will settle the dust. Now for
something to settle the water.

The Bodie Free Press
November 1879

Martha Delilah Cain, 1890s
Mono County Historical Photo

My mama was born Martha Delilah Wells in Nevada's first white settlement, Mormon Station, in 1861.

By the fall of 1879, my father, James Stuart, twenty-five, and Martha Delilah, eighteen, had bought a house in Bodie, and settled down to a married life together. It was a union only death would break.

Papa had so many business deals it is a wonder he could keep them all going—but that is how Papa always was, going at his life full-tilt. With a good head for business and knowing when to trust and when to back off, he just kept moving up and up.

Papa formed a gold mining partnership with his buddy from his Carson City days, Joe McGuire. They took out a lease on part of the Standard claim that was lying idle. Sure enough, Joe was a good partner with an excellent nose for mining. The two of them hit a rich vein right off. Why, it was so very good the Standard people took back their rights after about six months—but no matter, Papa cleared close to $100,000 for his share, and that was after everybody else got paid off.

Lots of men would have gambled, drank, or otherwise lost such a wonderful sum. Not Papa. He saw the whole picture of the mines at Bodie—which meant plenty of folk got rich investing, plenty of miners barely broke even, and plenty wasted time jumping from one place to the next. Papa planned to stay with Bodie to the bitter end. He felt if one lead didn't pan out, surely the next one would—you must just stick to what you know best and set about letting others do what they might, so you could both make a good living. Papa never was one to "just get by." He felt he owed Delilah much more than that.

So with his gold mining profit, he invested in some promising gold stock. Some money went to the bank and paid off the house, and there turned out to be plenty to invest in something that was catching fire back around Tahoe and Virginia City—small steamer ships that couldn't make a living hauling more people to California, (since train traveling was so much quicker and cheaper) were building up, sitting idle, and being auctioned off for taxes.

Papa knew that there was always real money in timber for the mines and the town was wood-poor, and that the best stand of suitable trees could be located south of the big Mono Lake. Trouble was that the stand of trees was cross-country from Bodie and there were no roads from the forest to the town. Freighting men, Papa included, saw Mono Lake as a water road, and already barges were being used to float the huge timbers to and from the sawmills. Barges worked well in good weather, but a steam engine-propelled boat would make the whole thing quicker and safer.

Papa decided to invest in the *Rocket,* sent up his bid, and next thing you know, he was a ship captain. Only the *Rocket* was up in San Francisco Bay, and Papa was in Bodie. Papa probably didn't even waste one night's sleep over this small detail—after all, he was a twenty-mule-team freighter. Everything can be moved if it is in small-enough sections. So sure enough, the newspapers reported that engine parts were starting to show up at the express office. And shortly thereafter, mechanics were tightening bolts and forging, and painters were giving the *Rocket* a new coat of paint. Several business fellows went down to the lake to see the first send-off, and Papa tried to get Lila to come along as well to share in his big moment—but you know how stubborn Mama can be. She told Papa (I have heard this story a thousand times): "No, Jim, I will be just too busy on Thursday to see you off, you go along with the menfolk, and I'll see you at supper when you have the time."

Papa always had a twinkle in his eye and made Mama just blush, for this is when Mama was "laying in;" or getting ready for the arrival of a child. Mama was not going out much at all, and she had even hired a

American Culture at the Turn of the Century

The history of childbirth remains one of the most hidden of subjects, because in the 1800s this phenomenon was not discussed in public. Certain tidbits can be uncovered, but most of the history is buried with the women of the time.

Childbirth in urban and rural America of the 1800s was very dangerous, with between 1 and 1.5 percent of all births ending in the death of the mother from "exhaustion, dehydration, infection, hemorrhage, or convulsions" (www.digital history.uh.edu/history online/ childbirth.cfm). Children often died as newborns, and one in ten children often did not reach the age of five.

Due to these high risks, pregnancy was regarded by most mid-nineteenth century women as a very private affair, and most relied upon female relatives and midwives to get through it. Women were expected to continue all their normal household chores, and a popular superstition of the time was that hard work led to easy labor.

In 1900, less than 5 percent of women gave birth in hospitals. Children were born at home without the assistance of medication or doctors, until the late nineteenth century when ether was introduced to help with the pain. Medication led to male doctors being called in, but most births still occurred in the home.

Women were for the most part expected to get right back to their chores within days or weeks of the delivery, depending on whether the woman could afford to lay abed. With the expansion of the national railroad system, which enabled the goods of one section of the country to be easily transported to another, modern urban homes had conveniences such as running water, gas, electricity and sewer systems, but most homes still relied on outhouses and tin bathing tubs, filled with heated water from the kitchen stove. Vegetables, meats, and dairy were more easily obtainable as the refrigerated railroad car was connecting seasonal items to customers. Tomatoes and citrus fruits began to be more a part of the meat and cabbage diet of Americans. Sears and Roebuck and Montgomery Ward's mail-order clothing helped to create access to affordable fashions. The bustle and corset were still popular with the leisure class of women, but poor and middle class women did not copy these styles, which were unsuitable for housecleaning and childrearing. Women, especially Western women, became more active and played tennis, croquet, bowled, and bathed at the seashore and at the nation's lakes. Bicycles were very popular, and became the dream of every child. George Eastman developed the box camera. Women began to go onto college, were more likely to have their own social and political opinions, and were active in helping the poor, promoting temperance, and concerned with child protection laws. Workers began to fight in earnest for the eight hour day.

young Chinese girl, Pearl, to come in daily to help out with the house chores, like the carrying of the water and the laundry and bringing up the firewood for the stoves.

Even so, Mama was never one to put her feet up during the daytime. She had no end of things to attend to. Like all the other married women in town, Mama got up in the dark and lit the kerosene lamp beside her bed. In winter, the house would be very cold as she would dress. Of course she started with her under-camisole of soft, often washed white cotton, pulled on long stockings and long cotton pantaloons. Next would come an under-slip that reached the ground, and then her dress, long-sleeved and of a dark color, usually blue or grey. Over the dress she would tie an apron, which might conveniently have several pockets for her to carry a cloth handkerchief. Delilah would quickly gather her long hair in a bun at the back of her head and fasten it with long metal pins so it would not come undone. The only variation was that in summer her dress might be heavy, dark cotton, whereas in winter it would be wool.

Mama would not awaken my sleeping father, yet. She would go downstairs and light one lantern near the stairs and several in the kitchen. The morning sky pressed dark and frigid on every window, but the light glowing against the drawn curtains would show the world to which we were about to awaken.

The stove must immediately be attended to; the ashes were banked at night, to make the relighting in the dawn easier and keep a residual of heat in the house. It was Mama's duty to bring in the kindling wood, but it was Papa's responsibility to chop the logs into kindling-size pieces. Next to the stove was a box to hold several hours of cooking wood. The fire lit, the kettle must be heated for coffee, and usually she would cook a hot grain cereal such as oatmeal. Often eggs, or leftover meat, bacon, or ham, might be served. Sometimes buckwheat cakes were made, served with molasses heated up on the stove. James Stuart was very fond of maple sugar, as it so reminded him of his home in Canada, but it was very expensive, and we had to watch our pennies, especially in our family's early years.

Now Delilah would go back up the stairs, and make sure that the heat from the downstairs was sufficiently warming the bedroom. She would lay out Papa's clothing that she had cleaned and pressed the day before. Papa would dress and perhaps shave with the warm water Delilah brought up to him, and then he would cheerfully come to breakfast, set out for him in the warmth of the kitchen. The dawn was now in full display and some of the lamps could be trimmed down, and one or two saved to counter the evening's darkness.

Each morning, while Papa thoughtfully ate his breakfast, he shared snippets of the world of business with his wife. He described his associates with a humorous style that could always get Mama to smile. He also always managed to compliment her on the taste of his meal. In his line of work, Papa might be off to arrange a shipment of timber from as far away as Twin Lakes and Bridgeport, or the opposite direction to the Tioga Sawmills, and Mama was expected to wait faithfully until his return. These quiet moments in the kitchen, exchanging plans for that day and hopes for their future, became the strength of the relationship they shared to the very last of their days. Papa knew that when he walked out the door, he must first give Mama a hug and a kiss, as it often happened in his

A young lady has been discovered who blushes, goes to bed at nine o' clock, eats heartily, speaks plain English, respects her mother, doesn't want to marry a lord, and knows how to cook. She must be one of Edison's new inventions.

–The Bodie Chronicle

June 28, 1879

...it will hardly be denied that an average the (Western) women of today are physically superior to what they were a few years ago, when tight lacing and similar destroying customs prevailed. Young women take more exercise than they formerly did, they ride and walk more, and are in the open air.

–The Bodie Chronicle

February 28, 1880

Robert Collyer says that a woman who is not fit to be a poor man's wife, is not fit to be any man's wife.

–The Bodie Chronicle

July 24, 1880

Such rules as the following will be found profitable in housewifery:

1. Rise early, have your meals at regular hours, and be punctual in engagements.

2. Keep your house scrupulously clean and regularly aired every day.

3. Assemble all your family regularly, morning and evening, to praise and thank God for his goodness.

> *4. Be kind, be quiet, be cheerful, be forbearing and forgiving.*
>
> *5. Be just and generous.*
>
> *Never use inferior articles of food. Buy the best flour, lard, bacon.*
>
> Mary Ann Mason, The Young Housewife's Counselor and Friend. 1875

business day that he might not return until midnight, or even not until lunchtime of the next day. Mama was always Papa's first concern; he shared all his dreams with her first, and Delilah always felt confident that all things could be discussed with him.

Although some modern conveniences had come to Bodie and more would arrive, in the cold winter of 1879-1880, housewives' duties were constant and very physical.

Water for all household needs involved buckets and much carrying, fetching, and lifting, even when it came from the water-man's wagon. The water-man drove about the town, driving a long, slightly narrow wagon, with long wooden staves horizontally forming a long tank. The linear slats of the cylindrical water container were bound with strong iron bands. The drivers of these water tanks seemed always ready with stories about the doings of the families on the next street over. All warm or hot water must be heated at the kitchen stove, which was more lifting for Mama and the other housewives.

Plumbing could be as easy as a drain that emptied out the back of the house or as primitive as using a bucket to fill and carry out doors to dump. Many drainpipes were lead, the cheapest metal, and easily worked.

Floors, wooden or carpeted, were swept daily with a stiff broom, and the dirt was swept right out the door onto the immediate yard. Carpets were carried outdoors in good weather and beaten with a big wire "rug-beater."

Beds might be shaken daily to keep out critters, but laundering linens by hand in winter's freezing temperatures was mostly a waiting game for the warmer days of spring and summer. Laundry involved heating water on the stove and lifting this large heating kettle to a tin basin and wringing and scrubbing by hand, followed by open-air drying on a clothesline set up in the yard. Sheds were often built attached to the back of the houses, to accommodate winter laundry washing and drying areas. The kitchen, with its warm air from the stove, would also be converted to a drying area.

The housework demands kept Delilah more than occupied, and combined with shopping for groceries in an age before refrigeration which limited the shelf life of items needed which necessitated more frequent visits to the butcher. Some items were delivered; such as milk and water. Often dry goods such as flour, potatoes, lamp oil were available in very large and heavy packaging, so these might be delivered.

Cooking meals involved many more hours of the housewife's time.

Although clothing was becoming more available ready- made, this was primarily for men's suits , so that most probably Delilah still did sew most of her own dresses, and she would certainly spend a great deal of time sewing clothing for her new baby. Bathing and personal hygiene also presented distinct challenges in the primitive frontier town of Bodie. Most families took care of these needs in the quiet privacy of their own home without the conveniences of running water and sewers. As in the big cities like San Francisco, public bath-houses were available.

Bodie Well
(Photo by Author)

GUIDE TO THE PUBLIC
Which if carefully observed, will prevent their being poisoned
by the use of impure water.
PURE SPRING WATER
The undersigned is prepared to furnish Pure Spring Water in
the Town or up on the Hill, from Green Street Spring, at the
most reasonable rates.
THE ONLY SPRING WATER
Available in This Vicinity
All orders left at Boone & Wright's store
Will be promptly attended to.
MOUNTAIN SPRING WATER CO.
Richard Brown, Agent.

The Work of laying drainage pipes still continues.
The Daily Free Press
Tuesday, June 1, 1880

On Monday morning sort your clothes. Have ready three large tubs; then take a quart of good soft soap (or dissolved hard soap); add to this twelve tablespoons of the mixture from the jug (slack 5 pounds of best lime with 5 pounds of sal soda in two gallons of boiling water, let it settle, and strain the liquor into a large jug; then pour on the lime and soda two gallons more of water, stirring it well; allow it to settle again...to this mixture add a pint of spirits of turpentine and an ounce of sal ammoniac) . Mix it well with the soap... soak your clothes for a half hour...have three tubs of clean water ready...put the clothes now in the boiler, as soon as boiled, rinse them in the clean water, rinse, starch and hang out...All this may be done in the course of the morning, and the colored and flannels may be easily ironed in the same afternoon...

A mistress of a house should inspect every apartment daily: see that the whole is swept, dusted, aired, and divested of cobwebs.

Pantries and store-rooms should be cleaned out at least once a week. Shelves, where china and glass are kept, should be carefully dusted. Closet, cupboard, and pantry doors should be kept shut and locked, so that the cats, rats, and mice be excluded.

Bedrooms should be aired daily; beds at least once a fortnight in the sun.

Chimney's should be swept down in winter daily, before the fires are made, as far as the ordinary broom will reach, particularly in kitchens; and care should be taken to burn them out on rainy days.

Clothes-lines should be taken in every evening; the weather will mold and rot them.

Custards and puddings should invariably be made of new milk; otherwise it will be apt to curdle.

Milk should be set in a cool place in summer, where it will be safe from dust or insects, but uncovered.

Cream should not be churned till it becomes thick, slightly sour, and at a temperature of sixty-two; then it will yield its butter quickly, and of the best quality.

Churns should be aired daily, and well scalded with boiling water after used.

Butter should be washed before being used for cooking sauces or puddings.

Salt meats should be soaked in cold or milk-warm water before being broiled or fried.

Fish, meats, and poultry should be well and carefully washed.

Rice should be carefully divested of any gravel or sand, and washed in several waters before boiling.

Salt should be covered in a dry place.

–Mary Ann Mason, 1879

FAMILY SUPPLIES
WEST & BRYANT
Are daily in receipt of
Choice Family Groceries!
Comprising many new
Rich Table Delicacies!
Our stock is now the best selected in
Town and we invite the atten-
tion of our customers and the
Heads of families in general
To the following list:
French Mushrooms,
Choice Point Reyes Roll Butter
And
Fresh Ranch Eggs
Received Daily
Goods Delivered Free of Charge
Liberal Discount to Cash Customers.
WEST & BRYANT.

All the latest newspapers, daily and weekly, and sheet music,
at M. M. Gillespie's
Garden, grass and flower seeds at Bodie Pharmacy.

Bodie Market/ Mono County Historical Society Photo

For stationary, pipes of all descriptions, cutlery, notions, soap of all kinds and jewelry, go to Hyman's cigar store. For a genuine Havana cigar, such as Star of Cuba, American Seal, Souvenir and other choice brands, which are too numerous to mention, you will find them I. Hymam's. For assorted socks at $1 50 per dozen, French and Scotch snuff, Florida water and Lubin's, go to Hyman's, Main Street, next to Wagner's saloon.

Genuine English Muffins every morning at the Parlor Eating House.

Central Market,
No. 34 Main street, Bodie, Cal.,
SUMMERS &CO............PROPRIETORS
Wholesale and Retail Dealers in
BEEF, MUTTON,

VEAL AND PORK.
Corned meats and sausages of all kinds-
Meats delivered free of charge.

FOR DRY GOODS, FANCY GOODS,
Yankee Notions, Jewelry,
Hats and Caps, Boots and Shoes,
Gentleman's Furnishing Goods, Etc.,
Go To
SILAS B. SMTH'S
Corner Main Street and Standard Ave.
BODIE, CAL.

By definition, Yankee notions consisted of items like pins,
needles, hooks, scissors, combs, small hardware and perfume.
The Yankee Peddler carried goods in an oblong tin trunk slung
on his back by a harness or a leather strap.

The History of Direct Selling (MLM Business Opportunities Blog)

New Firm and New Store.

Messrs. Elliott and Barnum will in a few days, open a new
store in the FREE PRESS building for the sale of fresh vegeta-
bles, fruit, fancy groceries, etc. These gentlemen are well known
here, and it is their intention to keep the very best of everything
in their line. Fresh goods will arrive daily by fast freight and
express order to supply the market. The place is one of the neat-
est in town, and nothing will be left undone by the firm to make
the business extensive and successful.

The Bodie Free Press May and June 1880

THE BODIE BATHS
Main street, opposite West and Bryant's
FRANK C. GILL,....................Prop.
These baths have lately been repaired and
Water from the Bodie Water Company introduced
The Water is
SOFT AND CLEAN
The only water fit for bathing purposes in this city.
At The
OK BARBER SHOP
MAIN STREET, BODIE
(Opposite Bodie Chronicle Offices
Will be found the
FASHIONABLE BARBERS
And HAIRDRESSERS
Of BODIE.
LADIES and CHILDREN'S hair cuttings
A SPECIALTY.
MOORE & ANDERSON
The Bodie Chronicle
June 7, 1879

The disposal of human waste in Bodie and the West, while a point of historical reality, has never been fundamental to any public records.

In a settled community such as Bodie the subject, although not often discussed, had to be planned to avoid the unpleasant smells and mess associated with human habitation.

The method of choice in Bodie is memorialized to this day in the sprinkling of wooden outhouses that are a testimony to the best the times had to offer.

"The typical frontier outhouse was basically an oblong box, three to four foot square, and approximately seven feet high. Built into the back wall of the outhouse was a two foot high wooden box, with an oval-shaped hole cut into it. The wooden box functioned as a toilet. Fancy outhouses had lids that covered the hole... Though some settlers sprinkled lye or lime down the hole after use, there is little that could be done to control the smell, which became unbearable in hot weather. In lieu of late night trips to the outhouse, most settlers kept chamber pots in their house, which were later emptied into the outhouse." http://www.pbs.org/wnet/frontierhouselife/essay5_2. html

Like so many other great inventions, the Chinese are credited with the originators of 'toilet paper.' A traveler to China in 851 A.D. records that the

"Chinese do not wash themselves with water when they have done their necessities; but they only wipe themselves with paper"(wikipedia.org).

Many various materials are mentioned in Wikipedia such as rags, wood shavings, leaves, grass, hay, sand, moss, water, snow, corn husks, to do the job we today take so for granted.

A British paper company coined the term "Therapeutic Papers" (T.P.!) for boxed sheets available in 1880, and in 1879 the Scott Paper Company began selling the first toilet paper on a roll. The outhouses of Bodie remain, but all else that occurred there-in shall be left to the imagination.

Bodie
(Photo by Author)

CHAPTER TEN:

"SOMETIMES WIN, ALLE TIME LOSE"

THE STORY OF A HIDDEN PEOPLE IN PLAIN SIGHT.

*Dealing in stocks is a fascinating but dangerous business. As Captain
Bob, of the Paiutes, sagely observed in regard to his experience in gambling,
"sometimes win; alle time lose!"*

–The Bodie Free Press
July 11, 1878

y name is Suzy Bill. I am a Kuzedika, what you call the Paiute tribe.

I was born on the morning after a full moon rose over the first wild iris bloom. Mother welcomed me with a song of joy, and the whole family attended the water blessing performed by my mother's aunt, who had reached the time of her life when she remembered the old ways more clearly than what happened yesterday.

My father thanked all of the stars and the wind and the lava-carved land for my birth. His father was away down the far valley, but a message was sent and Grandfather thanked the land for the happiness of a gift of a small girl child.

From the beginning, I was wrapped in softness harvested from the earth and carried in a beaded basket on my mother's back as she happily went about her days, washing the clothes and cleaning the house of the white family.

My first memories are of reflections of the green ryegrasses doing wind dances in the clean, rushing waters that the mother-land had provided for the people. The sun winked at me every day as I bobbed and turned in a waltz with my mother's chores. After she left the soapy bubbles of the white people, the moon shed a slender light on our cooking fires, always surrounded by the kind faces of my kin, dark eyes sharing whispers of comfort. My first steps came long after the snow of my first season had melted on the hills that cradled us all around. My feet were wrapped in soft leather, my body protected with bright cotton cloth. Mother and Father and my aunts and uncles laughed until they cried to see my first stumbles in the velvet meadow, with the azure sky reaching down to give me a gentle lift. Surrounded by kinfolk—sleeping, waking, working, cooking, gathering the wild willows, Suzy Bill (as my name is pronounced by the Americans), of the Kuzedika Paiute, opened her eyes and looked at the world that remains. I stood above the town of the mountain diggers. My older brother John told me it is the place they call Bodie and that the wood house dwellers said that the time is 1885. My brother knew many things regarding these strangers; he spent many times with our uncles, harvesting and turning the earth for their children to eat the gifts the rains provided. I was in awe of the greatness of the Granite Mountains, and revered the giving waters of the Mono basin—the wooden houses looked very small in the palm of the

I was a very small child when the first white people came into our country. They came like a lion, yes, like a roaring lion, and have continued so ever since..."

Our children are carefully taught to be good...We are taught to love everybody. Our tenth cousin is as near to us as our first cousin; and we don't marry into our relations. Almost all the girls were named for flowers...we talked about them in our wigwams, as if we were the flowers, saying "Oh I saw myself today in full bloom!" Many years ago, when my people were happier, they used to celebrate the festival of Flowers...All the girls who have flower names dance along together...some girls are named for rocks and are called rock-girls, and they find some pretty rocks which they carry, each such a rock as she is named for... if she cannot she can take a branch of sage-brush, or a bunch of rye-grass, which have no flower. A girl is never forced by her parents to marry against her wishes.

Sarah Winnemucca, Domestic and Social Moralities/
Life among the Paiutes

The Owens Valley Paiute used... a cradle... that consisted of a flat rectangle or trapezoid of basketry, vertical and horizontal rods being lashed together...equipped with a hood... which was used by the Yokuts and Tubatulatal tribes as well, indicating trans-Sierra diffusion. All of these tribes indicate the infant's sex by a design on the hood, a zigzag designating a girl, a row of horizontal dashes a boy. This seems to be of Shoshonean origin.

–Mojave Desert.net/ethnography
Indian Culture (Owens Valley Paiute)

For sewing and basket weaving the Owens Valley Paiutes used cactus thorns. Men wore buckskin shirts. Women wore buckskin dresses. Tattooing was not practiced, and women allowed their hair to hang loose from a part in the middle which was sometimes painted red. Men and women wore buckskin moccasins when traveling, and rabbit skin blankets for protection against the weather.

> *"I do not know how we came by the name of Paiutes. It is not an Indian word. I think it is misinterpreted. Sometimes we are called Pine-nut eaters, for we are the only tribe in the country where pine -nuts grow."*
>
> Sarah Winnemucca, Life among the Paiutes

Tina Charlie 1944 Mono County Historical Museum

Mother Earth's hands. Perhaps these strangers would leave soon as the elders hoped. My brother never disagreed when the aunts and uncles spoke. This would be worse than anything—but his eyes as he regarded these lopsided dwellings revealed that hope must not wait for the departure of these strangers from our land, but must reside in acceptance of the decision of the elders to coexist quietly. Let the lands defeat these graspers, they said. The land and the Kuzedika were patient, and struggled to feed their people.

My life as a girl is a memory of winters of snow and summers of the sun and wind kicking up the dust. My mother did washing and cleaning, and very often I was her helper and co-worker. We thought only to get a few coins to bring back to my father. He provided all else for us. He would make trades with our wash money for flour, coffee, sugar, and sometimes candles.

The white people did not own us, and we liked to joke about their strange manner —we knew some feared us still. We enjoyed that, in a kind way. But white men were a tremendous worry to my mother, and she took great pains to avoid them, and would try to act "stupid" when she encountered them, acting like she did not understand them.   But Mother did understand and she did not wish to ever encounter a white man alone. We stayed close to our aunts and cousins, if we did go into the town of Bodie. The aunts all had tales of what these coyotes could do to any girl who ventured out alone, and I had a great fear to be that poor lost girl. I took great pains to hide my face from the white men, and never them see any part of me.

Away from the town, we were all very free. The moon rose over our granite brothers, the great mountains, and the waters of melted snow were clean and cool on the hottest days. Mother cooked over a tidy fire her entire life. In the fall and spring all the women would gather the willows and there were many happy hours when we dried them, cleaned them carefully, and then each would weave the basket pattern that blended our lives with the land.

When I was very small, we had a great scare. If the white people ever wanted anything from us, they would send a message to our captain. Captain Bob was now very old, and mostly he sat beside the fire of his wife and let his son John take care of any difficulties.

It seemed that the whites wished to send a person to count up our numbers, and sent this in a letter a long distance to the government. This caused a great deal of discussion, and even Bob got up from his comfortable place and made a talk with us.

"I remember the last time these people counted us," he said. "I was much younger and was still thankful for the birth of my second son. I was very happy that day, so I felt generous. I gave the man my name as Captain Bob, and I brought a sizeable group with me. The man was interested in the ages, and who was married and who was not. The man did not ask for our names. I just told him what he seemed to want. I made things up—but he seemed very pleased and we received some flour and some nice cloth. My wife made many meals and we all had new shirts."

My cousin Minnie spoke next. "I remember the day after the ducks numbered so great that as they flew away they darkened the very skies. It was a warning. On the next day my two older children, one boy and a beautiful girl, were suddenly missing. They had been at the fire for the early meal, and at the night they were gone. I searched high and low, my tears so many I was a ghost of myself, and my husband suffered as I could not even cook for him. Then a piece of paper came and the words were read to me—the whites came and took the little precious ones! The man with the gun and the law said 'You should be very grateful, we took them to the Christian school, and they have new shoes, and read from books.' I am an old woman and my children are vanished. We will lose all our children to these Christians who value shoes and papers more than a mother's love and care."

"In 1859, the discovery of gold and silver in Northern Paiute territory along the Virginia Range attracted thousands of settlers to the area. The Comstock Lode shifted the demographics of their territory within a few months as a minority population of a few hundred whites exploded into a majority of many thousands… this onslaught of white domination was sudden, complete, and irreversible. The opportunity for natives to respond and resist was nearly gone before they could even comprehend the threat…non-Indians, seeking rapid profits…native hunting and gathering grounds were seized, miners cut down groves of pinion trees to shore up mines, streams were diverted for flumes, ranchers seized grasslands…"

–Rosemarie Stremlau, *Portraits of Women in the American West*

"Trade and barter eventually developed between the settlers and the Kuzedika Paiute. When the whites first entered the Mono Basin in large numbers in the 1850's, the Kuzedika avoided them completely, temporarily abandoning the north and west shores of Mono Lake. Gradually, however, they returned, and tried to live as they had before. But the continuing presence of the whites- first the hordes of miners at Monoville, then the large numbers passing to and from Aurora and the settlers occupying the fertile spots in the basin- forced the Kuzedika into a slow process of adaptation to new conditions. Finding it increasingly difficult to procure their traditional foods, they became more dependent upon the white settlers. The Kuzedika had always been traders; it was a simple step, although not a painless one, for them to broaden their trade network to include the whites.

As time went on, the Kuzedika began to trade their labor for goods. It is impossible to say when they first began to work on the white farms, but by the mid 1880s, Kuzedika men were indispensable hands during the sagebrush clearing, fence building, threshing and winnowing the harvested grain.

–Thomas C. Fletcher: Paiute, Prospector, Pioneer

Twice a year, in the time of the white butterfly, and again when the young quail ran neck and neck in the chaparral, Seyavi would cut willows for basketry...Every Indian woman is an artist, sees, feels, creates, but does not philosophize about her process...

–Mary Austin, The Basket Maker, 1903

The characteristic Owens Valley Paiute coiled basket is bowl shaped and bears banded designs in red and black...sometimes oval in shape...the large conical carrying basket , used in gathering food, seeds, etc, and in transportation of various goods, is characteristic of the Great basin peoples where it is well made and is decorated with banded designs. Another twined basket developed in conjunction with their use of wild seeds is the flat, fan-shaped, tray like winnowing basket. Distinctive of the Great Basin tribes and correlated with their need of transporting water in their arid environment was the pitch coated, twined water bottle. For coiled basketry... the Owens Valley Paiute employed three... or two... rods of willow (Salix Sessilfolia Nuttall). For the base or ground color, the wrapped element is a willow splint: for the black design, it is fern root of some aquatic plant or of tree yucca...as to the meanings of the designs...they were not religious or symbolical: they did not represent abstract ideas…they were merely designs, used primarily for their aesthetic value, and were given names such as Flies, deer foot, rattlesnake markings etc.

Basketry was to the tribes of California what pottery was to the Southwestern tribes—used to boil water, by lifting hot rocks into water tight baskets…

–Mojave desert.net/ethnography

All of the children were very scared! Who would disappear next? Perhaps the counting man would tell these "Christians" my name! A thousand times I saw the white faces saying "Suzy, Suzy, where is that Suzy Bill?" How stupid I was to ever trust the kind faces of their women! Now I knew why Grandmother always kept her head so low when these intruders were near. I could not sleep, I was so very afraid—I knew that I would surely die if they took me away from my dear mother, father, and brother.

My brother finally put an end to my nightmares. "We must try harder to be worthy of our parents' love," he said. "I will ask father for more time to go with him to work at the sawmill south of the blessed waters, and you will stay here away from the town and learn cooking from Auntie, and weaving baskets from our grandmother.
"

My heart was filled with happiness to think that instead of leaving, I would spend more time with family. Already my brother and I had started to think as one, and this was the beginning of our long bond—as our elders slipped further back, away into the lavender haze of our ancestors, we realized that the days ahead would be our fight, and that a new path was now before all the peoples of the shining blue mother and the gray granite father. It would be a long walk, before the next gathering of the wildflowers.

"The White Man's Road"

Ever since the Americans decided to move west into the Indian Territories, tears were shed around the tribal campfires.

Some tribes gave way and displaced other peoples, some fought to the last man and woman could stand, and some, like the great Paiute nations, chose to coexist, and stoically shelter their culture while intermingling with the Americans.

The federal government's Indian policy sadly reflected the ignorance and greed of many unscrupulous politicians and businesspeople, even though many others were motivated by kindness. The settlers themselves lacked any true understanding of the long and honorable cultures of the native peoples of the West. Often fear and economic desperation motivated them. Christianity was the nail in the coffin of any hope for coexistence between these peoples—religion for all its benefits, actually held Americans in a headlock of morality and social respectability. Anyone outside the pale was forever to be shunned and could count on public ridicule and isolation.

The American expansion into native lands is littered with federal policies that favored the white citizen over the Indian. After the decision to form "concentration camps" for native peoples on the most worthless land gained popularity, and the philosophy of "civilizing" the native people came into fashion, education of the young was followed suit. Francis Walker, as the commissioner of Indian affairs, has the unsavory reputation as the voice of this program.

*"In his 1872 report as Commissioner of Indian Affairs, Walker argued that "the only hope for salvation of the aborigines" is" the white man's road"... "they must yield or perish", the Indians must forsake savagery for civilization by **going to school**, joining the Christian church, and learning to farm like the white man."*

"Richard Pratt, would lead the Indian boarding school movement...in 1878 as an officer of the United States Cavalry guarding Indians in St. Augustine, Florida. He became a mentor, teaching industrial and agricultural skills,...convinced that Indians could only survive if they gave up their own values and adopted those of the white man...it was necessary to kill the Indian and save the man (by assimilation)... and in 1879 founded the most famous of the Indian boarding schools at an abandoned army post in Carlisle, Pennsylvania."

socrates.bmcc.edu/bfriedheim/shape west

For many of the Indians, boarding schools created a profound identity crisis, caught between Indian and white culture with no clear sense of who they were.

"Babes in the Woods"

Yesterday Captain Bob of the Paiutes was playing poker and got raised out on a very good hand. He had quit the scene of gambling, on the sunny side of Smith's store, and was standing looking at a squaw and her papoose when a FREE PRESS reporter entered into a conversation with him on subjects bearing on the Paiutes, social and public life. Bob said he had but one wife and was never married but once, expressing himself as well satisfied with the choice he had made years ago. While on the subject he pointed out an elderly Piute who was playing at the fascinating game and had three dollars before him. "His name is Joe," remarked Bob, "and he has been married three times." He said he was the father of sixteen children and all but two were living. The first wife died in Truckee about ten years ago, and left him with five children. The next woman he married was from Carson, and they were blessed with six children by the union. "She got killed on the railroad; heap cut up" was the simple story of her fate. Joe's present wife was pointed out and proved to be a fat woman about thirty years of age. She was surrounded by four children and another one was watching the game of poker. Bob says there are seldom any divorces in his tribe and but little infidelity. The Captain was willing to take two bits for all this information, but did not grumble at the receipt of an orange.

–The Daily Free Press
Wednesday, June 9, 1880

Judy Daniel

Paiute Cowboy 1880's Bridgeport Mono County Historical Society

CHAPTER ELEVEN:
TOOT! TOOT! TOOT!

*The Bodie Railroad and Lumber Company, under the energetic manage-
ment of Superintendent Thomas Holt, is making rapid progress with its
railroad, to the timber south of Mono Lake. Already nine miles of road have
been graded, and about three hundred men-two hundred whites and one
hundred Chinamen-are constantly employed. By next week the company
will be ready to employ a hundred more men. A wagon road six miles in
length has been constructed from the Lake to the site of the sawmill, the
timbers for which are all cut, and the frame for which is ready to be raised.
The engine and the boilers for the mill are now on the road between Bodie
and the mill. Nine miles of road are required to carry it from Bodie to the
plains, while in a direct line it is but four miles. On the grade from Bodie
over this first nine miles 35-pound steel rails will be used, and on the plain
35-pound iron rails. There is no doubt but that the road will be completed
and in running order before the snow flies.*

–The Daily Free Press
June 23, 1881

As surveyed and built, the distance of the railroad was 31.74 miles from Bodie station to Mono Saw Mills. Sidings were located at the terminal and at Warm Springs- eleven miles north of Mono Mills—and at Lime Kiln— twelve miles south of Bodie station. Elevations were 8500 feet at Bodie station, 6426 at Warm Springs, and 7346 at Mono Mills.

Emil Billeb, Mining Camp Days

Mono Lake Lumber Yard
G.L. Porter &Co, Proprietors
Yard on Green street west of Main, Bodie
Rough, Clear
AND
Dressed Lumber,
DOORS, WINDOWS, MOULDINGS
SHINGLES, PICKETS,
And in fact everything kept in a first-class
Lumber yard.
Lumber received daily from our mills at
The Lake

LOCAL INTELLIGENCE.

Settled. We are glad to know that the creditors of the firm of G.L. Porter &Co have decided to let this well known and enterprising firm work out their differences by resuming business. At a meeting of their creditors held on Thursday evening. Messrs. Bryant, Ambler and Kane [James S. Cain] were appointed assignees. The business will go on as usual, and the firm has ample assets all, in due time, will get their money. Captain Porter has done much toward advancing the prosperity of Bodie, and no man in our midst is more deserving of consideration at the hands of those in business relations with him. Had it not been for the unlooked for depression in mining affairs this season this firm would have been on the top round of prosperity.

–The Chronicle
August 28, 1880

Jim Cain was able to buy into the Bodie Railroad & Lumber Company, with Thomas Holt, the superintendent of the railroad. J.S. Cain & Associates later leased the railway lumber yard in Bodie and became agents of the railway.

–Mono County Historical Society, 2007 Newsletter

Cain Family, 1890s
Mono County Historical Society Photo

apa loved to tell me about the first years after he and Mama had settled in Bodie. It was always my greatest joy to have Papa's attention. I eagerly quizzed him on the old days. "Why, Doll, you would never guess how much things in Bodie have changed! In the wide-open days, claims were being filed daily, and there was work for well over a thousand miners. Nowadays the gold fields have narrowed down to three main mines, which every schoolchild can recite: the Bodie, the Standard, and the Syndicate."

As Papa relayed the story, he explained that many businesses, who had in the flush times been doing very well, the restaurants, boarding houses, and grocery stores, now had fewer paying customers. As the mines closed down, and prospectors moved onto new camps, many residents were forced to follow if they had no other work. This caused many businesses to fall on hard times and as more and more customers owed money to these establishments, and could not pay what they owed, it became like a sad game of dominos. Sadly the most generous businesses, being owed a great deal, now could no longer pay their own bills, and had to close down.

In the long cold days of the Bodie winter, if a man did not have work that was guaranteed, it meant he had better get moving to someplace where he could find it.

For those of us that stayed, we noticed the rowdy ne'er-do-wells left first. Good riddance, Papa said, and most who stayed agreed.

Fact of the matter is, the good times got better *after* the boom days of 1880-1881. Sure, mines began to close one by one, and the glory days thinned out considerably, but families that had put down their roots in Bodie had managed to hit ground water, and for these folks life went on like an old melody, just vaguely audible but very pleasant all the same.

The dance halls faded as their tarnished doves flew away. Most of the saloons were boarded up and the drunks drifted to other towns, but there was always a friendly place to get a drink with the boys—one could find good times and still make it home to the family for a decent dinner. Our stores were still well-stocked, and the hotels still put up the travelers. The Miners' Union Hall continued to hold Saturday night socials, where miners' wives served lemonade and ice cream and the band played merry tunes deep into the night. The school house was crowded with children, poetry was recited, geography memorized, and the girls held hands playing rhyming games in the dirt yard.

Boys, young and old, still searched for old Will Bodey's grave, always thinking that he had taken the secrets of fabulous wealth with him on that frozen day in 1859, and his bones would lead to a defrosted treasure just waiting to be found.

The Standard newspaper still fought elaborate verbal duels with *The Free Press*, while *The Chronicle* moved over to Bridgeport; all the while trading poisonous jabs until all three faded into the dust, and Bodie was left with just one small newspaper, *The Bodie Evening Miner*, which served all the needs of a family town that mostly let the world outside alone.

For my Papa, times got better and better. By the time my little brother James was coming, Papa was partner at the Bodie Bank. Soon, he owned the bank.

SODA WATER!
GINGER ALE!
SARSAPARILLA!
CREAM SODA!
R.A. Leale having purchased the entire plant
Of the Pearson Brothers and removed and set it
Up on Main Street, is now manufacturing all of
The above drinks in a most superior article
These will all be sold at the lowest percentage.
Orders from the outside solicited, which
Will be promptly filled by return stages.
Send orders to
R.A. LEALE
Bodie. Cal.
The Bodie Evening Miner
August 4, 1890

E.F. GIBSON
FRUIT AND VEGETABLE
MARKET
UNION MARKET BUILDING,
(above the Post Office)
BODIE
Receiving daily, by express
Fresh Fruits and Vegetables
Of all kind ,in season.
The best of WINES,

LIQUORS,

CIGARS,

TEAS,

SPICES,

COFFEES,

CANNED GOODS,

NUTS,

FRENCH CANDIES,

ORANGES,

LEMONS,

LIMES,

SMOKING AND CHEWING TOBACCO.

FRESH EGGS always in store,

FINE FAT POULTRY always in the coop.

Goods promptly delivered.

Orders from the County solicited.

HIGHEST PRICES PAID FOR FRESH

COUNTRY PRODUCE.

The Union

Bridgeport, Feb. 23, 1884

THE BODIE STORE

WM. ROUSH, AGENT,

Is the place to buy supplies of all kinds. No better

Assortment in the market.

Bodie
(Photo by Author)

MOYLE BROS.
Dealer in
STATIONERY, CIGARS, TOBACCO
FANCY GOODS & NOTIONS
BODIE, CAL.
The Bodie Evening Miner
Aug. 4, 1890

OCCIDENTAL HOTEL,
Main Street, Bodie, Cal.,
N.W. BOYD, Proprietor
The OCCIDENTAL will be kept strictly
First class in all departments.
The Table cannot be surpassed, as none but the best

Cooks are employed.
The rooms are all heated and well kept.
The Bar is unexcelled in the quality of liquors and
Cigars kept on hand.
The Bodie Evening Miner
Aug. 4, 1890

Bodie Bank
Mono Historical Society Photo

Still if you were to ask him what it was he did all day, he would get a gleam in his eye and tell you: "Why, I am a gold man, through and through, and, if you can keep a secret, just about to hit pay dirt."

Fact is, Papa was in on just about every job in Bodie at some point: he was a Wells Fargo Express agent, on the school board, the head of the waterworks, a major player in the railroad and lumbering businesses, an investor in the Booker Flats Racetrack, a freighter, a horse owner, a stable man—you could name anything and Papa had a share in it.

Sam Leon, and many other Chinese residents of King Street, greeted him as a friend. Captain John, the last local chief of the Paiutes, sat at our kitchen table and was served coffee. Townspeople looked up to Papa. Children were afraid of the man in the starched shirt who always wore a suit coat and a proper town hat. Half the town worked with him or for him at one time on one or another of his ventures.

Bodie (Photo by author)

Temple Saloon
Is first class in all its appointments
The Finest
WINES, CIGARS and LIQUERS
Free Billiard Parlor. Lunches of all
Descriptions always on hand.
Courteous treatment.
Delury & Garcia.   *Props*

Chronology

1860s: The town of Bodie grows slowly. The Bodie Bluff Consolidated Mining Company (later the Empire Company) brings miners to Bodie and by 1864 a permanent mining community is established.

1875-1877: The discovery of a rich vein of gold ore begins the "Bodie Rush."

1877-1882: The Bodie District reaches its peak production.

1883-1890: Mines begin shutting down and Bodie experiences a steady decline. By 1890, only two mines are in operation.

1890's Bodie resident and property owner J.S. Cain introduces cyanide mining and electricity, sparking a small revival of mining in Bodie. This revival consists mostly of reworking of old mine tailings and low grade ore dumps. Only a few hundred residents of Bodie remain.

1910-1920: Bodie's population drops from five hundred to less than one hundred.

The cyanide folks looked him up when they came up with their idea to get the gold out of the waste of the early days. The electric generator engineer had Papa on his team of backers, and the first long-distance, water-powered electricity coming in a straight line from Green Creek to the Standard Company in Bodie came to reality because of men like my papa.

The big world swirled about, but in our town, life flowed like the "crick"—that would be Bodie Creek to you outsiders. Sometimes we would have a tremendous

snow year, with July still sending snowy frozen gifts from the clouds. The creek full of crystal clear water flowed up until mid-August before it went underground. Other years, we were barely let out for summer school break when the creek was nothing but dried up mud holes. But the creek bed was never, ever dry and gone for good. And like our "crick," our town of Bodie never completely died.

Lots of other towns loved to hail our demise, but through the years we continued on, with fewer hotels, a smaller school population, and a whole lot less of the bad men, a group most folks never did miss.

For me, Jessie Delilah Cain, better known as Doll, life was a very pleasant journey—you could say the times were perfect for little girls growing up on the American frontier.

My older brother, David Victor Cain (christened David for papa's father, and given Victor for Mama's mother Victoria), we all called Vic. He was two-and-a-half years my senior. Vic was just the image of our wonderful mama born a boy, they looked so much alike! So you know he did all things proper, like mama, and was such a good student that the teachers all just loved him. He never missed his assignments, and always stayed behind to help straighten up. The girls all loved to sit next to him, since he would always share his lunchbox and never tease. Vic wasn't a sissy; he could be a fighter if he had to. The thing was, Vic could talk most other of the boys away from using their fists. Still, I never saw him turn his back on a bully. Mama always said it was because Vic was born at the beginning of sunny summertime, in June, that he was such a pleasant fellow.

Of course, you know I am going someplace with this description of my brother. Well, just as Vic was mama's son, I surely was Papa's daughter—I hope you don't think worse of Papa on account of me. I surely had my mama's dark curls, but other than that I was just the mirror of Papa. Now a boy with good manners is a joy, but a girl with the manners of a boy, well, that could cause a mother some amount of grief. Oftentimes this was the situation between Mama and me. I surely never meant to misbehave, and when mama would again sit me at the piano to practice and to think over my sins, I was always most properly regretful and determined to do better next time one of my wild ideas would get hold of me.

Papa could always get folks to gather around him, and I shared his talent, since I seemed to be always getting other children in all sorts of scrapes and adventures. Their mama would tell my mama that their children would never have got into these ventures if it weren't for me, and my ideas. Why, my head some days would just be swarming with plans, and even though I would promise Mama to attend to only the most ladylike of endeavors, somehow I would just completely forget her earnest pleas.

Perhaps it would help those unfamiliar with our Bodie for me to draw out a bit of a map. It is full of the places that are of interest to me and my playmates, and shy of those sections of Main Street that interested adults. If you take a look at the map you will see a very dense square of family dwellings right around my house on East Fuller, right on the intersection with Green Street.

You can see the schoolhouse several blocks south, right on the creek, up Green Street. And I do mean up, since our street was in a bowl of sorts, with the top of Green quite steep in both directions. If I walked west on Fuller Street I would shortly arrive at the Metzger household, where my best friends Maud and Mabel lived with their many siblings. To get to them, I would pass the Methodist Church and the lumberyard and sawmill. All the upstanding families had homes in this quiet section of town. Continuing from the Metzger house, there were several choices for destinations. One could follow Mr. Metzger up Union Street to his workplace at the Standard Mine. Most of us children were strictly forbidden to explore some of the offshoots of Union Street as it reached Main. This included King Street, where the Chinese lived, and other streets that seemed to have more drinking establishments than was proper for children to view. If I went the other direction, the houses were fewer and quickly turned to more open space, below the cemetery grounds and out to the Booker Flats raceway where we had many delightful social events every Sunday. There were always more stables, and farm-like buildings to the east of our house. If I went past the schoolhouse I could walk onto Wood Street, with its many small cabins where the miners and their families were set in rows leading over to St. John the Baptist Catholic Church. If we had permission to continue, this way would eventually lead to the Cottonwood Canyon, which had many rural homes spaced among abandoned mining ventures. Now, if you didn't turn on Wood Street but continued on Green, the climb was very steep, but there were many fine residences and boardinghouses that climbed all the way up to the Railroad Station, and the huge Porter Lumberyards, which had a wonderful shallow pond that froze every winter and where we could ice-skate to our heart's content.

I surely got more time sitting at the piano thinking over my sins after the Christmas Papa bought Vic and me brand-new Victor safety bicycles. Things stayed tame enough when the snow kept us on the boardwalks, but with the early spring we had that year, the whole world opened up for a youngster pedaling in the fresh air of the Bodie hills.

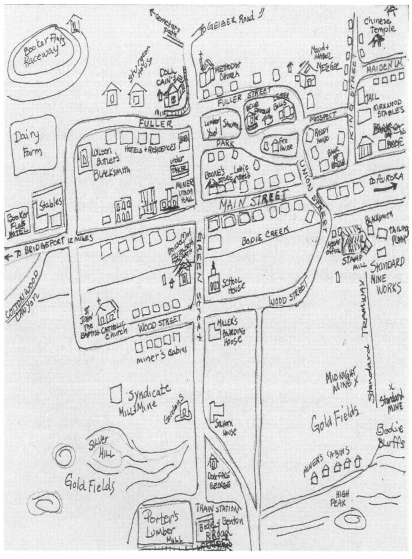

Sketch of Doll's Bodie by Author.

The Bicycle

The safety bicycle is a type of bicycle using a diamond frame and invented by John Kemp Starley in 1885. Safeties are cycles with two identically sized wheels with a chain- driven rear wheel, and as the name implies are more easily maneuvered, making them popular with females.

Sewing machine factories had the right equipment to manufacture these new bicycles, and offered the opportunity to make a profit.

The Rover Company was building the safety bicycle in England, and the Victor Company of Philadelphia was turning them out by 1886. With the invention of air-filled (pneumatic) tires in 1889, the safety bike was comfortable and affordable.

The 1890s were known as the decade of the bicycle. Once prices became reasonable for most people (under one hundred dollars for a good bike) a social revolution occurred. Young people found themselves able to pedal past their own neighborhoods, and a generation of women traded their corsets for bloomers to make riding easier. Susan B. Anthony said that the bicycle has done more for the emancipation of women than anything else in the world.

Paper Dolls

A paper doll is a two-dimensional figure drawn or printed on paper for which accompanying clothing has also been made.

The very first paper dolls were hand-painted figures and costumes created for adults, possibly done by dressmakers to show current fashions. Early European paper dolls depicted actors and actresses (Ellen Terry, Lily Langtry), the German Royal Family, and the House of Windsor. *Godey's Lady's Book* was the first magazine to print a paper doll in black and white, in November 1859, which was attached to a page of costumes for children to color.

Publishing Companies, such as McLoughlin Brothers and the smaller company Peter G. Thompson, published paper dolls in the 1880s. They were sold for five to fifteen cents per set and had names such as Dottie Dimple, Lottie Love, Jessie Jingle, Bessie Bright, and Pansy Blossom. Often the costumes would be carefully glued onto the doll with tiny drippings of wax, and later on, tabs were drawn on to fold the cut-out costumes to the dolls.

I tell you Mama sure gave Papa a talking-to after the first time I was late to supper because my bicycle got a flat and I had to walk who knows how far back home.

Papa did favor me, his Doll. The story came out that it was actually two of us, my best friend Maud and I, who were riding together, and it was her bicycle that got the flat, and we traded so she would not get punished for being late, and after getting the story, not from me, but from that gal's grateful papa, Papa stuck up for me with Mama. I still spent a week with no bicycle privileges, and it was beautiful weather to boot, but Papa said it was very noble of me to help out a friend.

I can't say that I ever thought Mama was wrong in any way, and to this day I hold her to be a lady without equal—but sometimes when I pedaled hard up to the top of Green Street just to turn about and come flying downhill, I surely did feel a sense of light-headed freedom that was more delicious than the best ice cream on a hot Bodie summer's day, and with the wind tearing at my proper skirts, I did feel a bit wicked. I came up with some of my best plans while riding that bike. Sometimes not riding got me in trouble as well.

One day, being too hot, to really enjoy a good ride, I was trying to think of someplace dark and cool, where the heat wasn't so very bothersome. I was sitting on the front porch with Maud and her sister Mabel. Checkers seemed boring, and paper dolls were chosen as the plan for the afternoon. We had our paper dolls set out on the porch, thinking it was cooler in the shade. Our plan was building a house for our dolls. We had mama's kitchen scissors, and all sorts of beads from my broken necklace, and wonderful bits of ribbons and small cuts of cloth.

We were having a very rare moment of peace from my two younger brothers, as Mama had walked over to Auntie Cherrie's house with these two, allowing the boys to romp with Cherrie's children while Mama and Auntie chatted over a sip of tea. My older brother Vic was supervising us, but I happened to know that his lunch had made him very sleepy, and while he said he would be reading upstairs, most probably he was doing that with his eyes closed.

I got to thinking about what paper would be just right for our paper house, and next I was thinking about those papers that the Chinese folk like to burn at funerals and holidays. And all of a sudden it happened into my head, that the Chinese cook had mentioned how very soothing the inside of the Taoist temple on King Street was, and I told the girls to come on, that I knew just the place to get some very desirable paper, not to mention get out of a broiling-hot Bodie afternoon. If the girls had really known my intention was to enter the temple, I am sure their collective good sense would have prevailed.

Riding our bicycles down Park Street, we turned at Union Street until we were suddenly on King Street, a place even we knew, at ten years old, was forbidden, although that may have been what pushed us that day. In Bodie, as across California, the Chinese separated themselves into their own little communities, for protection from the hatred many just seemed determined to demonstrate and for cultural comfort, as the Chinese valued their own ways and felt at ease surrounding themselves with as much of their motherland as possible. The Chinese washed our clothes and worked in our kitchens, so they had daily contact with us, but to see three little white girls dressed in gingham dresses pushing bicycles, you would have thought we were from the moon.

Amazingly, no one stopped us, even when I leaned my bicycle up outside and made to enter the temple, with Maud and Mabel following like lambs, so scared they did not dare leave my side. The building looked almost ordinary on the outside and the roof line was curved more than I was used to, but it was inside the door that the world of Bodie fell away.

It was indeed very dark, and refreshingly cool. There were many candles burning, all glowing like tiny stars lined up along every nook and cranny and softly illuminating statues of persons in long gowns with sad, beautiful faces. I saw red and pink papers tucked by the candles, and the fragrances wafting about the room were some I truly cannot describe.

There was only one very old Chinese gentleman sitting to one side of the room. I was not sure he was not a statue himself until he said to me very softly "Can I help you, my child?"

I tried to be brave as I answered him. "My friend Gin, our cook, sent me, as I was hoping for a fortune to be read to me and perhaps, if you please, some bits of paper if you might have extra."

Such a kind man, this gentle person was, and he did not scream "Liar!" He only indicated for us to sit down. He smiled and brought out from his long sleeves a bamboo cup with many little sticks.

"I will try to assist you, honored children. First let us ask guidance from the Ancestors …" He tossed these bamboo sticks at the base of the statues and lit many sticks of incense, and even more candles. The bamboo pieces had strange designs scrolled upon them and the man seemed to study each one, as if he were reading.

His face grew more and more serious as he studied the sticks, glancing at these three white devil children sitting in his temple, a place reserved for his kinsmen. As the minutes inside the temple extended into what seemed an eternity, my bravery melted into an pool of foolish regret; I think we all thought we were surely to be taken captives forever, never to see the safety of my front porch ever again, and all on account of my stupid whimsies.

I already missed my brother's scolding, and my mama's sad face when she heard of my loss floated into my mind, and it was almost more than even I could bear. I think I could hear Maud crying, and Mabel was simply frozen in fear—and then after what seemed a very, very, long time, the priest started to speak, first to Maud, then Mabel, and lastly to me. As he spoke melodiously to each of us, he honored my request and would bow and offer out bits of shiny red, pink, silver, and gold papers.

"You will marry well, and have many babies," he said to Maud. Maud stopped sniffling, and she carefully took the bits of papers. "You will study at a far place and be lonesome for your family, but at long last you too shall come back home," he said to Mabel. She had the presence of mind to mumble "thank you kind sir," as he offered pink and silver papers with his words. Now he paused here for another eternity. After I thought I would just faint, he turned his almond eyes to me at last and spoke very clearly in the cool darkness. "I see a porcelain doll wearing a red silk gown—take care to not shatter it, tossing it too high in the air!" He actually extended his hand and offered a small paper-formed flower to me! I know I took it most gratefully, but my manners were fairly blown away. I could not speak a single word. Our eyes were, I am sure, as large as teacups. None of us dared to breathe. The old man smiled slowly. "Is that all?"

"Oh my, yes!" we almost screamed out, so glad to be dismissed; we walked as fast as we dared out the red doors, and jumped on our bicycles, the bright, hot air of Bodie fairly blasting us as we raced up to the Union Street cutoff and to the safety of home.

Mama thought it ever so queer that I simply threw myself at the piano for many days on end after that and refused to go outdoors to ride, even asking to do extra mending chores, until Vic started to give me a curious, knowing look.

The paper doll house we did finally make was like none other, I must say, and other girls always asked us, wherever did we gather all those queer paper wall hangings?

Our always-silent and ever-polite cook, Mr. Gin, laughed out loud as he served dinner next evening, something that was very remarkable to Mama and Papa, but thankfully not discussed with me.

If you ever looked into my top drawer you could smell the light fragrance of far- off lands, but all you would see was a small, perfectly-shaped, not faded at all, flower.

Bodie Museum
(Photo by Author)

I must admit I had scared myself a bit, and I behaved like a perfect young lady for almost several weeks after my journey to Chinatown. I always wondered how that old man knew my name was Doll, and however did he know I really did have a red silk pajama set?

Life returned to its routines. August came and school reopened. I would get up as soon as mama called and put on one of my school dresses, not my best ones that I wore for Sunday school, but always very clean (Mama made sure of that), with cotton stockings in warm weather and dark wool ones as fall turned the Bodie air chilly.

My very favorite dress was my light blue cotton, sailor-style, with a dark blue matching coat that fit snugly. I had a straw hat with bluebells on the rim. My hair was very long, and Mama would brush it every morning and twist the ends about her hands like magic, and I would have long dark ringlets like mama used to wear. My face had fringe bangs cut straight across my forehead. Mama usually tied a matching ribbon to my dress in my hair if I wanted it.

I always had calf-high button black leather shoes with a flat sole for school. I also had a very special pair that Papa had brought me from Virginia City—white calf leather, with a small heel and red laces. Oh, I loved those shoes! I was almost afraid to wear them for fear of messing them.

The proper length of my skirt was a constant worry—at ten it was mid-calf, but now that I was twelve it was just above my boot, and Mama would tell me I was growing like a weed, and would catch up to Vic if I wasn't careful. Mama was only five feet tall and her demure stature was very feminine. At twelve, I was as tall as she was, and it seemed I took after Papa again. I was never plump, and could always eat lots without fear that I would bust out of my dresses.

The one thing I always took after Mama in was about how particular I could be about my clothes. I could just spend hours poring over the Butterick fashion magazines, checking how the sleeves were getting fuller with every year that we went into the '90s. Mama was such a clever seamstress, and she could sew and alter old dresses to look the latest styles. Mama always took time to add ribbon to all my better dresses. It was a small nod to my good behavior. Mama encouraged my interest in the fashions we would see in the books from the notions department at Silas Smith's store. Mama, as a married lady, may have had to wear darker, proper colors than she would have wished for, but she just loved to dress me in all the new, bright pastels, plaids, and even polka dots. Many nights I would sit with mama after dinner was cleaned up, and we would plan out my dresses. Together we cut, sewed, and mended. I always remember how carefully Mama held her sharp sewing scissors. I loved to sort through her embroidered sewing basket, color-matching the wooden spools of threads, and counting out buttons from her tight-lidded jar, already neatly stowed in her basket of goods.

Papa would read the newspaper, every so often reading out loud to us tidbits of news. He enjoyed reciting the names of folks who attended the wedding last Sunday at Bridgeport, and what gifts each family brought. He would laugh out loud to read that a certain family gave a rooster. Papa thought that a rather silly gift, as who could use another noisy rooster? And those other folks gave a black horse. Papa thought a horse always a fine wedding gift, and who would not agree?

The fire would be lit if the weather showed any chill. In Bodie, that was usually ten months out of any year. Vic entertained himself indoors with the latest dime novel. His particular favorites were the popular Seaside Library stories. These short works had real Western boys as heroes, and had exciting illustrations. Vic would have a smile on his ever-cheerful face, and he would laugh out loud at the wonderful times the heroes had. Little Stuart and Jimmie usually got out their tin trains and their toy soldiers. They had already learned that if they got too noisy they would be scooted off to bed. Wisely, they managed to keep their games to the far end of the room, where Mama might forget their bedtimes. Time in our world stood still as we shared many wonderful evenings of quiet companionship. Bodie is forever linked to these peaceful memories we have as children born and raised there.

It seems that my good fortune from my adventure at the Taoist temple could only last so long before I just got into some new scrape. As with many accidents, it started out quietly.

One of my morning chores, now that Mama was raising four children, was to help get Papa's lunch basket all together, on those many days Papa traveled very far from home on business. Mama would set aside leftover tidbits from the previous evening's supper for me to organize and wrap up in a clean cotton cloth and place in a small basket—Papa favored roast beef and a small baked potato, and I was pleased to pack these up for Papa on this day. Vic usually got his own lunch together, but I always got to pack my own lunch pail—I was so excited to see a nice chunk of bread pudding sitting on the sideboard. Mama's bread pudding was a coveted item, and my friends at school would be so happy to share their lunches with me.

I wrapped up Papa's lunch, and then my own, just as Mama called out to me to help get Jimmy dressed, as he was now going along to school each morning. I guess I just got mixed up and accidentally switched Papa's lunch into my bucket and my precious bread pudding into his basket.

I got Jimmy squared away and, rushing now, I grabbed at the chance to walk to school a bit earlier than usual since Papa was walking past the Green Street school on his way up the hill to the train station. Jimmy would come along later with Vic, and I was free to spend some time alone with Papa.

One of his occasional duties was to catch the earliest outbound train from the station overlooking our town and journey to the end of the line at the Mono sawmill. Papa was responsible for accurate inventory figures, and this required an in-person visit from Papa to make sure that the trust of the investors was being protected.

Oh, it was a delightful walk, holding Papa's warm hand, walking along, as he told one of his funny stories. He hugged me good-bye at the school yard, and he no sooner left than the thought of that delicious pudding started to gnaw at my stomach, and knowing I had packed extra, I felt I surely deserved a bit now, waiting for my friends to arrive.

Oh! Imagine my dismay when I found potato where I had hoped to see pudding! Why, Papa did not even care for sweets.

The next thought in my mind was to save Papa from a disappointed luncheon. I could just barely see Papa fading over the crest of Green Street. I believed I could easily fix this little mix-up. I began to run up the hill as fast as possible, hoping to catch Papa. It seems I underestimated my ability, as Green Street is really very steep when you are running uphill. I was gasping for air by the time I reached the top. I got many stares from the workmen merely walking to their duties—but I was determined to catch Papa.

The railroad was not ever a passenger business, but simply a workhorse moving the much-needed timbers from the mountains south of Mono to Bodie's mines.

I burst into the station, much to the surprise of the older gentleman manning the counter. But he was all alone—no Papa!

I figured Papa had simply already boarded and could be still be waylaid to make the exchange of lunches. Without another thought in the world I stepped up onto the platform at the caboose and bravely entered the vehicle. I was just about to determine that again there was no Papa, when the whole vehicle took a very sudden move forward, an unexpected jolt sent me to my knees, and without any more warning I felt myself moving, rocking side to side as the little train picked up speed.

I gazed out the small window to the rear of the caboose and saw the station fading quickly as we began the steep descent down to Mono Lake! The grade downward was famous for its steepness, and hairpin switchbacks lent extra excitement to my now-very-empty stomach. I was so overcome with my predicament that I felt beyond tears—and I had been trying so hard to behave and be a responsible child for Mama and Papa.

Getting hold of myself, I remembered that the train would have to stop halfway to the Mono sawmill to fill up with water, near Warm Springs. Perhaps I could get off and move up the train to talk to the engineer. There, I found Papa perched up beside the engineer to boot.

Bless Papa! He simply turned and greeted me as if we had planned the whole thing as a father and daughter outing. "Why, so good to see you doing well, my Doll, and so soon after our walk—did you forget to kiss me farewell?"

Now I did decide to burst into tears and between sighs the story of bread pudding and potatoes came out and the engineer gave Papa a knowing smile, being father to three daughters himself.

I did not expect to be rewarded, but Papa was never one to sweat the small details. So he carefully left a message for one of the returning teamsters to give to Mama:

Not to Worry Dear Lile, Doll Is Safe and Sound and With Me. Will explain all Later, Jim.

And I was lifted up to sit with Papa, riding the locomotive with the brisk air in my face and one of the workmen's coats wrapped about me.

That was the thing about Papa—when I messed up he was always the first to look on the bright side, so even though I might spend some hours at the piano in

> *"Timber grew in the mountains some thirty miles to the south, on the other side of Mono Basin. A railroad would make this supply more readily available to the mines. In 1881 the Bodie Railway & Lumber Co. was organized. It constructed a three-foot-gauge line 32 miles to Mono Saw ills in the mountains south of Mono Lake. Here were set up railroad shops, lumber mills, logging camps and all that was necessary to serve as the center of a large lumbering and cordwood operation.(pg 35)... The railroad office building on the hill...was a solid two-story structure, well built to withstand the heavy storms and high winds that often buffeted the hilltop.*
>
> *The main floor was mostly a large room...it had a counter running along two sides, with the usual high desks and stools behind it...behind the main office was the kitchen...heat was provided by wood stoves...water had to be laboriously packed in buckets from the town reservoir on the hilltop..."*
>
> –Emil Billeb, Mining Camp Days

the following days, he never said a cross word to me then.

When we finally reached the mills, Papa had business to attend to. He safely placed me in the kitchen with a very large bearded man who was very busy preparing lunch for the workers, but not too busy to serve me a very delicious slice of cake he had baked that very morning!

The Mono Sawmill was its own little village, its huge machinery operated by a score of engineers and sawyers. There were also a team of lumberjacks and teamsters cutting and hauling gigantic trees to the mill, to be made into usable lumber and cordwood. There was a bunkhouse, which was open for free rooming, and three meals a day were available for a daily charge of one silver dollar. Local ranchers supplied beef and produce, and there was even, of course, a small saloon for the men to unwind at the end of the day.

After my bit of cake I was allowed to wander a bit, as long as I stayed well clear of the workingmen. It was most dangerous working conditions, and I did not dare have any more adventures that day.

At long last, Papa finished his business and we climbed back aboard the returning train. This time we snuggled in the closed caboose. It was dusk now and very cold. I really lost track of time, I know I slept soundly and I barely remember Papa carrying me into the house, well into the dark night.

What Papa told Mama I do not know—but I certainly was not allowed to walk to school unattended again. Vic again got the job of babysitter, and he was very careful to not ever let me out of his watchful view. Good old Vic!

School was out for summer. The hot weather would just flatten Bodie. On alternating weeks we would be rattled with deadly hot winds, followed by days of still heat that made us just beg for the winds to start up again. Most of the families had lots of children, and it being too hot to send them outdoors was just driving all the mothers cranky.

It was a custom to go picnicking to the lower Cottonwood Creek to sit by the water and under the aspens, down below the Booker Flat Racetrack—but in the summer, often even this was not much of an escape from treeless Bodie. Often families would plan to go camping over to the beautiful Virginia Creek, halfway to Bridgeport, with those great waters always flowing deep and cool, with lots of shade trees. Twin Lakes, above Bridgeport, was also a desired destination, with its famous ice house where ice cream was the specialty. Also common was to take the advice of the Paiutes and head for the Sierras in the hot months. Oh, the weather could be just fine up under the pines, temperate all day and not freezing at night, but plenty cold.

The mighty Yosemite Park was a very desirable destination, and could be reached by buggy ride from Mono Lake and up the canyon right past the Scarvino family goat ranch, to the mining town of Lundy. Yosemite already had a long history as a tourist spot; in 1864 it became "Yosemite Grant," after 1872 it was a state park, and in October of 1890 a national park. Resting overnight at Lundy's hospitable Lake House hotel, it was possible then to arrange for a well-guided pack and horse ride up the canyon and crossing over to the Tioga Creek Canyon. This first part of the pack train ride was breathtaking and a very adventuresome journey. With steep switchbacks cutting back and forward along a rocky trail, views of the great Mono Lake would peek-a-boo suddenly out from the towering pine trees.

At the very top, the trail met up with the much-more-easily-traveled so-called Great Tioga Sierra Wagon Road, right below the Tioga summit. From here, the horses could enjoy relatively-level traveling across Yosemite's rim, past Lake Tenaya and Tuolumne Meadows, all following an excellent road into the Yosemite Valley.

My dear friends Maud and Mabel Metzger were very fortunate because their family would retreat up to Lake Tenaya just as the very hottest days of late July and August descended upon Bodie. Mr. Metzger worked up at the Standard Mine and welcomed peace from his brood of seven children, and encouraged his wife to join the many families from the Minors' Union who annually planned to make an exodus up into the cool trees.

Mrs. Metzger, kind lady that she is, invited me to come along with the family as their guest. Now, Mama in her full skirts was not too fond of camping outdoors, and felt Stuart and Jimmie too small to attempt it. Papa was always busy and Vic was helping out Papa, learning "the trade" that hot summer in Papa's downtown office. I had been moping about the house, miserably contemplating the absence of my two very best friends. It was too hot for bicycling, and no companions for paper dolls, playing cards, or just picnicking down under the cottonwoods.

Papa tipped the scale. He was just needed ever so urgently over at the May Lundy Mine; and what could be more perfect timing but that he must go just as the Metzger family would be residing at the Lake House Hotel, taking a day or two to rest on their way up to Tenaya Lake.

LAKE HOUSE
LUNDY, CAL.
(At the foot of the Lake.)
The best accommodations for
Transient and permanent boarders
And tourists.
A SPECIALTY OF THIS HOTEL
Is its Breakfasts and Dinner, served singly
Or to parties, at any hour.
A FIRST CLASS HOTEL
In every department. No extra charges.
PATRONS AND VISITORS
Have the use of Dancing Hall, Piano, Croquet   Grounds,
Boats, and Fishing Tackle.

Breakfast, from 8 to 11:30 A.M.
Dinner, from 5 to 8 P.M.
A.J. HOWE, Proprietor.

Lakeview Hotel

Mono County Historical Museum

I was beside myself with pleasure when Papa himself offered to take me along, right at dinner. Well, Vic rolled his eyes, but didn't properly utter a word, and for that matter Mama just straightened her back up and sent a swift look to the little boys, letting them know that although Papa might have won this one for their sister, they were not going to leave her for even a minute to go off horse-riding, tramping in mud, and catching cold for sure in those frigid Sierra lakes and creeks. Papa gave me a smile and told me that he must leave before dawn tomorrow, and I had best be packed and sitting in the buggy if I really did want to go.

Packing up for a camping adventure was, and always will be, my cup of tea. I got the most important items packed first—my water-colors, paper, and my flower press; my best and favorite doll, Mary Ann, the one I always took along when we would travel to visit folks far off, and her clothes; my almost new riding boots…

I was so well behaved all that afternoon Vic told me I was sickening. Oh! Nothing he could say would dampen my spirits. Off to the woods for almost four weeks—whatever could be more sublime? No little brothers, no scolding; I did feel a twinge of guilt leaving Mama to carry on at the house without my help. Although Mama was against the camping adventure on ladylike principle, she nonetheless spent several hours with me, packing up my last year's dresses and my old wool sweater and gloves in case it turned cool in the evening. Mama made sure to fold in the proper cotton undergarments, with lots of advice on how to clean them. Then, with a wink, she put in a pair of Vic's trousers—letting me know that it was "almost proper" for a young girl to wear these under her skirt while riding a horse, and much better than being immodest.

I had my own towel and handkerchief, my broad-brimmed, tall crown cowboy hat, and a straw one in case I might need one. Mama said more than once, please, child, don't come back with freckles, wear a hat at all times, and long sleeves to protect the skin on you arms. She almost got to start in scolding. She knew as well as anyone that once I got to the woods I was wild as any child, and she started a lecture of motherly proportions. But the little boys started up a tussle right then, and thank goodness for me, she turned to minding them and plumb forgot to make me promise to always be ladylike.

The next dawn, I was up before Papa. I had biscuits and coffee ready and packed away in the travel basket, and my knapsack was neatly stored already in the buggy. I had my older travel suit on. I was ready to go.

Oh, I cannot even tell the pleasure that ride was. I had always had a knack for horses and Papa would always set out as driver, but soon as the twinkling lights of town faded he would give me the reins. Papa was alert, sitting right beside me, but would soon relax, even light up a cigar and puff on it, telling his ever-entertaining stories. S

Such a lot of things Papa knew. He told me all about how the roads were built, and the troubles the stagers were having, and how the folks over in Lundy, fairly perched on the back of the grand Sierra, were making a go of it. "Mark my words, Doll, Lundy will outlast Bodie in a small way—the lake side would be fine for fishing and relaxing, and the city folks would even find some pleasure in the pure, snowy goodness of the place!" Papa was a man with big ideas, gold mining most of the time, but he made plenty of time to think about other subjects —the role of the gold mints, the value of modernizing the mills, the weather at Mammoth Mine as opposed to his Bishop ranch—Papa had lots to offer.

Thanks to Papa, I was delivered safe and sound to the delightful company of Mrs. Metzger, Maud, Mabel and several of the Metzger boys, all securely settled at Lundy Lake. We spent a busy afternoon laughing over croquet and tossing rocks in the lovely emerald lake, along with quite a few of our classmates, who were accompanying their families as companions to our party.

Papa spoke of the local Paiute families who themselves had been accustomed to this same trek to the high country. They showed good sense, escaping the hot winds and the rattlesnakes of the sagebrush country that bordered the Sierra Mountains, climbing up, up to the pine forests.

This was my first trip, and the beginning of what became one of my most favorite of traditions—returning to the mountain meadows perched along the glacial terrain. I need only close my eyes for my mind to see the steep canyons of granite rising above the lake all around, and to feel the crispness of the evening air, even in summer. The beauty of the place was only exceeded by its serenity. It seemed to quiet the thunder of our childish voices. The overwhelming stillness of the forest calmed my own constant chatter.

Papa, of course, saw our party off—we were perched on a fine string of pack ponies and had an impressive line of mules, with their canvas packs loaded, balanced, tied, and secured. We had the best wranglers assisting us, and quite a few skilled Paiute folks, packers, cooks, and firewood gatherers.

Mr. Moss was leading up our party. He owned the Overland Express, as it was called, and this long pack train of tourists anxious to escape was becoming a fine business. There was an excellent road up nearer the top of the Bloody Canyon pass, after we struggled through the lower elevations. Mr. Moss enjoyed pointing out the sights along the trail, mixing his stories with exciting tales of life in this area and fishing advice, and keeping a very close eye on his riders. Moss stayed especially watchful over the ladies, who might need his assistance with an unruly horse or a loose strap.

Our first day's journey was a big push for all of us travelers. We had to ascend several thousand feet to enter into the Tenaya Lake and Yosemite regions, and there is no other path but up, up, and up. The rock walls of the canyon above Lundy can only be described as vertical, rocky, and absolutely breathtaking. Truth be told, Papa had been setting me on my own pony since I was just a small Doll. My pony today was that terrific breed that lived in our high country, stocky and sure-footed—they got to know those trails like their own stables, and most seemed as anxious as we were to get out on the freedom of the trails.

I composed a letter to Mama in my head, cutting out some parts, so as not to worry her—like the cliff of carved granite we were just now inching along, of which I could look to one side and see a drop of many hundreds feet to the rocky canyon below, or about the mama bear and two cubs we surprised at the first creek crossing,

Gold Again

Although the glory days of gold prospecting and mining had just about faded by the 1890s, several small claims were still being worked besides the Bodie Bluffs, in the Mono-Inyo-Kern Counties. The town of Lundy grew up around the May Lundy Mines, and Mammoth had its hopes. Bennettville, named for Thomas Bennett, Jr. of New Bedford, Mass., president of the Great Sierra Consolidated Silver Company, was perched in a beautiful valley or cove at the base of Tioga Hill, 9,300 feet above sea level. It was sheltered on the south and west by the towering and somber cliffs of Tioga Hill, on the north by a timbered ridge between Slate and Lee Vining Creeks, and on the east by heavy timber. To connect Bennettville and its riches to the rest of California, a new wagon road coming from the western slopes was proposed, funded, and constructed. The expenditure for the fifty-six miles of road was $62,000 and, constructed largely by Chinese labor, took about one hundred days to complete in 1883.Alan Patera. Bennettville

The New Road

As the Great Sierra wagon road, now being built to connect Tioga District, on the summit of the Sierra, with the wagon and railroads of the San Joaquin Valley, is rapidly approach-

ing completion, it may be interesting to readers to see the details of the new highway. The distance between Bennettville and the railway at Oakdale is 123 miles…this is much less than the distance between Lundy and Carson…the new road is a good one, the grade generally being less than eight feet to the hundred, and on only two or three little pitches does it reach sixteen feet in the hundred. It is thoroughly well watered, and timber and grass are abundant…the route lies through the grandest scenery of the Sierra…

As the blasters on the lower section of the Great Sierra wagon road are now directly on the trail to Yosemite, and are setting off from 350 to 400 blasts per day their operations make it exceedingly lively for people passing that way on horseback…

Moss' saddle train is now making regular time between Lundy and Yosemite and is being liberally patronized.

A big forest fire is raging east of the Mono Valley craters.

Fishing in Parker Lake is said to be excellent. The Paiutes sojourn on its shores now…he fish at Lundy Lake are biting very satisfactorily at present and a good many messes are taken out by our fishermen…

Yosemite Notes: The weather has got warm and dry instead of cold and rainy; the roads are dusty instead of muddy…The excursion parties have come…and regular travelers are arriving daily…The Kelly line of stages from Sonora are bringing goodly number in their private carriages, with fine horses and accomplished drivers. The "Overland Saddle Train" arrived and…Miss Richards will accompany them, being the first lady to cross the mountains this season…Camping parties are arriving daily; there have been eighteen hundred visitors according to the hotel register here this season…

Miss Minnie Parkinson, operator for the Sierra Telegraph Company is a young lady with plenty of sand. Last Tuesday while riding horseback on the desert, a rattlesnake rattled in front of her. She dismounted, and procuring a stick, beat the snake to death. The rattlesnake was about four feet long and carried eight rattles and a button. Miss Parkinson has the "bells" filed away among her cabinet curiosities.

The graders on the Great Sierra wagon road entered the basin of the headwaters of Yosemite Creek a week ago…about 160 men, whites and Chinese are employed. They have about 30 miles of road yet to reach Bennettville, but it is believed the road will be completed by the middle or 20th of August. The road will run three-fourths of a mile along the margin of Lake Tenaya…

–The Homer Mining Index
July 28, 1883

Deer are numerous on Rush and Deadman creeks.
New potatoes from Mono Lake ranches are in market.
Five thousand sheep crossed by Mono pass, going west last week.

In The High Sierra

A brisk walk through the tropical climate, bright plumaged birds, and musical rattlesnakes of Mono Lake Valley, soon brought us to the fragrant groves, green meadows, crystal lakes along the eastern base of Mount Dana and Mount Gibbs... our first camp was at the head of the upper Horse Meadows,... just above the old Lee Vining Creek sawmill. From here...it was impossible to ascend...except up Bloody Canyon...Bloody Canyon possesses many attractive and many repellent features, and derived its name from the seemingly impossibility of any animal ascending or descending without bleeding its feet or legs on the sharp rocks. The cliffs or terraces cross the canyon at regular intervals from Walker's lake to McClure's or Mono pass on to the summit, a distance of four and a half miles. The lake at the foot of these cliffs is filled with both silver and salmon trout, which bit ravenously, especially in the creek which flows from the lake and meanders through the spacious meadow below. The cliffs are marked by many dashing cascades, thundering cataracts and beautiful ribbon falls...

–The Homer Mining Index
August 23, 1883

Well, you get the idea. They were fine tales for Papa or Vic, but I surely must not worry Mama. I decided my first letter to Mama would be a description of the wild irises, paintbrush and lupines—wildflowers that we sat among for our delicious lunch of fresh bread, peaches, and sliced roast beef from last night's dinner. We finished this delightful lunching and were off again. It was some hours to the site of our first night's camp.

I was so very sleepy at the end of that day's ride, I can just recall being wrapped in a soft cotton blanket inside of a canvas tent, after a cup of tea with biscuits and cold ham. Before turning in, the most glorious night sky of millions of stars set the backdrop for the smoky fires of the still-busy packers. The last memory I held onto was the tangy smell of pine, mixing with my dreams.

Next morning, there was a rim of ice on the water bucket. A quick breakfast dipped from a blackened pot of hot oatmeal thinned with sugar and canned milk and hot strong black coffee, and I was lifted up on my steady pony. His name was Carrot, and he was a friendly brute, switching his tail in the cold and eager to meet the sunrise up on the ridges above. We planned a shorter day, to give the ladies in the party a chance to rest a bit, and for us children to run about.

I was glad to have the warmth from my brother's wool pants under my skirt. I am sure my hair was as disheveled as other young folks in our company, but in the cold morning air conversations were short, and no one was commenting on our new outdoor fashions.

We rode seriously for a bit and were rewarded with the sun welcoming us just as we crossed over to the connection with the Sierra Wagon Road. There, the views from the top of the world became wave upon wave of mountain peaks, clad in snows of many years, the breezes carrying a moist pure flavor and the meadows becoming more frequent as we crossed creek after creek.

We were welcomed by our mule train, which had preceded us to set up the campsite, delightfully perched at the very top lake of Bloody Canyon. Here the fishing was excellent and all the children were supplied with poles by the thoughtful packers. We spent a warm afternoon falling in the so-cold lake, and picking ever-more-beautiful wildflowers as the fishing lagged in our girlish interests. I dearly wanted to know the names of all these strangely delicate flowers. Each was more special than the last and we girls started quite a competition to see who had found this one or that.

We were all so sad to pack up the next morning after this camp had been so hospitable to us—we had dined on camp stew, beef and new potato stew with dumplings, topped off by hot cocoa, which for whatever reason went to our young heads. We had many laughing fits over nothing before Maud got hiccups, and Mrs. Metzger looked a bit stern. Chastised just a wee bit, Mabel and I walked arm in arm, still giggling as we left the warmth of the camp-fire for our blankets, lovingly placed upon mats of pine needles.

As we came into the upper Yosemite Valley, our thoughts never tarried with any other place in this wide world. Oh, how the beauty surrounded us! Never have I experienced such magic as the first moments in Yosemite. Smooth, well-worn paths winding through forests of gigantic pines, rolling rivers softened by banks of ver-dant grasses, and all around, so close now you might be touching them, the mighty granite Sierra.

We easily reached our destination, the Tenaya Lake camp. The lake is truly an overwhelming jewel of topaz-colored waters, with one side a sandy beach, sheltered from the evening down-canyon wind, and the pine needles so thick our ponies' hooves made no sound as we arrived.

It was not really like a camp at all, but a small village of white canvas tents set on wooden floors that creaked delightfully as we ascended the ready-made steps. I was bunking with several of the girls from our school. Mrs. Metzger graciously let Maud and Mabel bunk with me at night, as long as we really went to sleep and cut out the shrieking at a decent hour.

Nothing will ever compare to the days in the High Sierra—the lovely lunches at the lakeshore, day-hikes up to the mountains, listening to the adults talk into the starry night of the days of their own childhood, reading aloud *The Swiss Family Robinson* until the light from the campfire proved too dim to continue.

Several of our party went on after some days residing at Camp Tenaya, planning to go on to the Valley of the Yosemite. But Mrs.

Metzger felt Camp Tenaya was enough of an adventure for her, and she did fret at the distance from Mr. Metzger. Her eldest daughter had stayed behind to care for him, and letters easily came back and forth, courtesy of Mr. Moss who would be in and out every day or so, bringing up tourist parties to join with us or move on as they pleased.

I, true to my promise to Mama, wrote every few days, and kept the family, according to Vic, greatly amused with my tales of frog hunting by moonlight, learning to roast pine nuts on fire-heated rocks, and the progress in the wildflower competition. It was the wildflowers that became the subject of a very contrite letter to Mama and Papa, not for my brothers to read.

I was ever so delighted with the colors and the variety of the flora of this mighty mountain camp, but after a bit, all the nearby flowers were gathered and pressed, and even drawn with my water-colors. Maud told me "you make me very cranky with your infernal gathering." She said this just as the whole family was to meet for lunch at the lakeshore. I planned to walk in the direction of the road for a bit, and since Maud would not come away, I took along Mary Ann, my faithful doll. I had a bit of bread from the kind Paiute female cook and a flask of tea, and I set out.

At first I recognized every tree and creek, but somehow I must have gotten turned about as I spied the purple of the sky pilots just above a tiny rock ledge, and after struggling to reach these, much higher up the rock face than I thought, I sat down. Taking a sip of tea, I felt the whole enormous mass of trees, rocks and the never-ending Sierra. I was lost.

I always kept Papa in my mind, I wrote him in the letter. I asked him what to do next and could just hear his voice telling me "Don't panic now, girl. This isn't serious yet. Sit down and plan out your next step." I hugged my dolly, Mary Ann, very thankful for her quiet encouragement, and said a prayer to the Holy Father. I scrunched up my eyes, not crying. I was not hurt in any way, I wrote to Mama.

BARNARD'S
YO SEMITE FALLS HOTEL
YO SEMITE VALLEY, CAL.
John K. Barnard.................Proprietor.

Central Situation, Beautiful surroundings
Ample room, abundant shade, right on the
margin of the beautiful Merced river, and
Immediately opposite and in full view of
The Yo Semite Fall, 2,634 feet high.
No one expelled for laughing out loud.
Accommodations as good as the best
And charges as low as the lowest.
Baths, Billiards, Bars, Barber and
Curiosity shops convenient, and Telegraph
And Stage offices in the Hotel.

Barnard's Hotel is the most convenient
to reach from this side of the Sierra, as
You cross the Merced river on a splendid
Iron bridge at the end of the principal hotel
Building, instead of fording the large and
Dangerous stream over the treacherous
Quick-sands in order to reach other hotels
Toward the lower end of the Valley—and

Judy Daniel

Moreover it is at Barnard's that
Californians delight to congregate.
  –The Homer Mining Index.
    September 13, 1884

I opened my eyes and lo! A girl, just almost my age, was standing just down a bit on the crop of granite. She stood very still, and if I was not so alone, I might never have noticed her.

It was surely Suzy Bill, who had come along with her mama, our camp cook and her papa, the packer who worked for Mr. Moss. Suzy was always quiet around me, but I knew her and greeted her as I was taught proper by Papa: "Good afternoon! I am so pleased to be seeing you!"

She called out, "Mama thought you might need a bit more of the sweet raisin bread with your tea, Miss Doll!"

And I knew that even as I had left the camp, Suzy had been sent to accompany me at a respectful distance, sent by the cook who had poured my tea.

I happily accepted Suzy's gift, and showed her my "sky pilot" wildflowers. She smiled very sweetly, and as we walked back to the camp together, she shared a very private comment that dark blue-violet flower was her special family name, and therefore her very favorite summer flower. Suzy was very comfortable among the great forest, guiding me carefully on a twisting path. Suzy told me that the sky pilot flowers were indeed rare and I was so very smart to have found them.

In my next letter I did not dare deny my terrible behavior in leaving the kind protection of Mrs. Metzger, and swore this behavior would never, ever, happen again. I was very concerned Mama might call me home if I confessed to my parents my grave error in leaving the camp. But for sure Papa would be told of my mishap, as he was told everything by everybody, and he had many Paiute friends. I knew it was best to own up and take one's medicine, as Papa would say.

I requested to Mama that I be allowed to give Suzy my last year's dress that I had with me, since it was too short for me anyway, and Suzy was just right for it, and would do well to have it. I felt very thankful that she rescued me from my flower crag, and led me back to the safety of Camp Tenaya.

It will always be a wonder to me how gracious Mama is. She would have something to say when she saw me, but all she wrote back was to tell me to include the petticoat as well, and make sure to tell Suzy's mama to stop by the house at her first convenience. There were other surplus items Mama herself wished her to have, as thanks to the sharp-eyed Paiute mother.

It was Papa who wrote back—a very stern letter, and I knew he had got the business from Mama at last for how he had spoiled me –this time really to within an inch of my life!

Oh! If you could but hear my repentances, uttered in the solemn cathedral of that mighty ancient forest, alongside the pearl of the Sierra, the blue diamond-shaded Lake Tenaya, white caps slapping the rocky shores, you could only know that I would always and ever be a credit to my family, no matter what temptation might call to me. As I looked about me I could only be thankful to be alive.

What a wonderful time it was to be a child and live these tales of golden days of Bodie, the last of the mining camps, forever beckoning us to partake in the feasts of our pioneer spirit, as strangely pure and clean as the icy waters of the Sierra.

Afterword

The people in this book are real. The only fiction involved is my narrative in relating them to you.

Elizabeth Butler, after our story, lived her remaining life in Bridgeport, California. Her brother Will Butler remained in Bodie, working as a blacksmith, until his death in 1896. Her brother Ben tried many business ventures in the California and Nevada areas and also preceded Elizabeth, dying in 1904 in Nevada. Elizabeth mothered all the children of the Butler clan, including those of her daughter Helen, who died in 1885. True to her nature, Elizabeth worked until the end of her life. The 1910 census lists her as doing laundry work from her home. She died in 1912.

Alice Beck lived with her parents in Bodie until her marriage to Harvey Boone. She and Harvey raised two daughters. The Boone family is remembered as long-time merchants of Bodie, and their store still stands at the corner of Main and Green Streets. As Bodie times declined, the Boones moved into Nevada. Margaret Beck lived with her husband Joseph until his death, having retired, after thirty years at the Standard Mine, to live in Bridgeport. After Joseph's death, Margaret moved in with Alice and her family.

Suzy Bill lived her entire life in the Bodie and Mono Lake area. Suzy married and bore three children, and her husband, like her father, worked as a packer in the Yosemite area.

Jessie Delilah Cain finished school in Bodie, and after graduation from high school she entered Mills College, where she earned a degree in music. After graduation, Doll returned to Bodie and worked as a clerk in her father's businesses, as well as serving for a time as postmistress of Aurora, Nevada, during that town's last boom years, 1905 to 1910. Doll met Emil Billeb in Bodie in 1909 at a social at the Miner's Union Hall. Emil had migrated to California from New York, and he proved himself to be an intelligent gentleman with a savvy financial ability that kept him employed in several of the Western gold towns. He was offered the position of superintendent of the Benton and Bodie Railway. Emil married Doll in San Francisco in 1911. They returned to Bodie to raise two sons. When the railroad went bust in 1917, the Billebs moved to San Mateo, California, where Doll's mother joined them in the early 1920s. Delilah Cain needed to be close to better medical care than Jim Cain's declining Bodie could offer. Jim eventually also joined the Billebs to live out his life in northern California, although he was always involved in Bodie.

Bibliography: BODIE *THE GOLDEN YEARS*

BILLEB, EMIL W. (1986)

MINING CAMP DAYS

        NEVADA PUBLICATIONS

        LAS VEGAS, NEVADA

        229 PAGES

BROWNE, J. ROSS (1865)

A TRIP TO BODIE BLUFF AND THE DEAD SEA OF THE WEST (MONO LAKE) IN 1863

        HARPER'S NEW MONTHLY

        REPRODUCED BY OUTBOOKS

        1981 GOLDEN, COLORADO

        72 PAGES

BUTRILLE, SUSAN G. (1998)

WOMEN'S VOICES FROM THE MOTHER LODE: TALES FROM THE CALIFORNIA GOLD RUSH.

        TAMARACK BOOKS

        BOISE, IDAHO

        271 PAGES

CAIN, ELLA M. (1956)

THE STORY OF BODIE

        FEARDON PUBLISHERS

        SAN FRANCISCO, CA

        196 PAGES

CAIN, ELLA M. (1961)

THE STORY OF EARLY MONO COUNTY. ITS SETTLERS, GOLD RUSHES.INDIANS.GHOST TOWNS

        FEARDON PUBLISHERS

        SAN FRANCISCO, CA

        166 PAGES

CALDWELL, GARY (1990)

MAMMOTH GOLD: THE GHOST TOWNS OF LAKE DISTRICT.

> GENNY SMITH BOOKS
>
> MAMMOTH LAKES, CA
>
> 171 PAGES

CHALFANT, WILLIE ARTHUR (1947)

GOLD, GUNS AND GHOST TOWNS

> CHALFANT PRESS 1975
>
> (REPRINT OF STANFORD
>
> UNIVERSITY PRESS)
>
> 175 PAGES

CHALFANT, WILLIE ARTHUR (1975)

COMMUNITY PRINTING

> AND PUBLISHING
>
> BISHOP, CA
>
> 430 PAGES

ENSS, CHRIS (2005)

HEARTS WEST: TRUE STORIES OF MAIL ORDER BRIDES ON THE FRONTIER.

> THE GLOBE PEQUAT PRESS
>
> HELENA, MONTANA
>
> 114 PAGES

ENSS, CHRIS (2006)

HOW THE WEST WAS WORN: BUSTLES AND BUCKSKINS ON THE WILD FRONTIER.

> THE GLOBE PEQUAT PRESS
>
> HELENA, MONTANA
>
> 127 PAGES

FLETCHER, THOMAS C. (1987)

PAIUTE, PROSPECTOR, PIONEER: A HISTORY OF THE BODIE-MONO LAKE AREA IN THE NINETEENTH CENTURY.

> ARTEMISIA PRESS
>
> LEE VINING, CA

123 PAGES

FREEDMAN, RUSSEL(1983)

CHILDREN OF THE WILD WEST

CLARION BOOKS

NEW YORK, NEW YORK

104 PAGES

GARCEAU-HAGEN, DEE (2005)

PORTRAITS OF WOMEN IN THE AMERICAN WEST

ROUTLEDGE TAYLOR

&FRANCIS GROUP

NEW YORK, NEW YORK

273 PAGES

GREY, DOROTHY (1998)

WOMEN OF THE WEST

UNIVERSITY OF NEBRASKA PRESS

LINCOLN, NEBRASKA

179 PAGES

HOPKINS, SARAH WINNEMUCCA (1883)

LIFE AMOUNG THE PAIUTE: THEIR WRONGS AND CLAIMS.

A REPRODUCTION

SIERRA MEDIA/CHALFANT PRESS

BISHOP, CA

PAGES

IRWIN,SUE (1991)

CALIFORNIA'S EASTERN SIERRA: A VISITOR'S GUIDE

CACHUMA PRESS

LOS OLIVOS, CA

144 PAGES

JOHNSON, SUSAN LEE(2000)

ROARING CAMP: THE SOCIAL WORLD OF THE CALIFORNIA GOLD RUSH

W.W. NORTON & CO.

NEW YORK, NEW YORK

344 PAGES

JOHNSON, RUSS AND ANN (1967)

THE GHOST TOWN OF BODIE AS REPORTED IN THE NEWSPAPERS OF THE DAY.

COMMUNITY PRINTING AND PUBLISHING

BISHOP, CA

117 PAGES

LOOSE, WARREN (1989)

BODIE BONANZA: THE TRUE STORY OF A FLAMBOYANT PAST.

NEVADA PUBLICATIONS

LAS VEGAS, NEVADA

246 PAGES

MASON, MARY (1875)

THE YOUNG HOUSEWIFE'S COUNSELLOR AND FRIEND: CONTAINING DIRECTIONS IN EVERY DEPARTMENT OF HOUSEKEEPING. INCLUDING THE DUTIES OF WIFE AND MOTHER

E.J.HALE & SON

NEW YORK, NY

ELECTRONIC EDITION

APEX DATA SERVICES

`   UNC-CH 2001

McGRATH, ROGER D. (1984)

GUNFIGHTERS, HIGHWAYMEN & VIGILANTES

VIOLENCE ON THE FRONTIER

UNIVERSITY OF CALIFORNIA PRESS

BERKLEY, CA

291 PAGES

McGRATH, ROGER D. (1978)

FRONTIER VIOLENCE IN THE RAS-SIERRAN WEST

DISSERTATION. UCLA

MERRELL, BILL (2003)

BODIE'S BOSS LAWMAN: THE FRONTIER ODYSSEY OF CONSTABLE JOHN F. KIRGAN.

NEVADA PUBLICATIONS

RENO, NEVADA

175 PAGES

MORSE, THOMAS I. (1990)

PHOTOGRAGHING BODIE: A PHOTOGRAGHER'S GUIDE TO THE GHOST TOWN OF BODIE, CALIFORNIA.

GLOBAL PRESERVATION PROJECT

SANTA BARBARA, CA

30 PAGES

NADEAU, REMI (1965)

GHOST TOWNS & MINING CAMPS OF CALIFORNIA: A HISTORY AND GUIDE.

CREST PUBLISHERS

SANTA BARBARA, CA

314 PAGES

O'BRIEN, MARY BARMEYER (2005)

OUTLASTING THE TRAIL: THE STORY OF A WOMAN'S JOURNEY WEST

THE GLOBE PEQUAT PRESS

HELENA, MONTANA

300 PAGES

O'ROUKE, EVERETT V. (1972)

THE HIGHEST SCHOOL IN CALIFORNIA

SACRAMENTO CORRAL

OF WESTERNERS

25 PAGES

PEAVY, LINDA

SMITH , URSULA (1996)

PIONEER WOMEN : THE LIVES OF WOMEN ON THE FRONTIER.

UNIVERSITY OF OKLAHOMA

PRESS

NORMAN, OKLAHOMA

144 PAGES

SCHUMACHER SMITH, GENNY, EDITOR (1978)

DEEPEST VALLEY: A GUIDE TO OWENS VALLEY, ITS ROADSIDES AND MOUNTAIN TRAILS.

WILLIAM KAUFMANN PUBLISHING

LOS ALTOS, CA

279 PAGES

SEAGRAVES, ANNE (1990)

WOMEN OF THE SIERRAS

WESANNE PUBLICATIONS

HAYDEN, IDAHO

173 PAGES

SEAGRAVES, ANNE (1994)

SOILED DOVES: PROSTITUTIO IN THE EARLY WEST

WESANNE PUBLICATIONS

HAYDEN, IDAHO

175 PAGES

SPRAGUE, MARGARITE (2003)

BODIE'S GOLD: TALL TALES AND TRUE HISTORY FROM A CALIFORNIA MINING TOWN.

UNIVERSITY OF NEVADA PRESS

RENO, NEVADA

247 PAGES

STARR, KEVIN (1973)

AMERICANS AND THE CALIFORNIA DREAM

OXFORD UNIVERSITY PRESS

NEW YORK, NEW YORK

494 PAGES

TWAIN, MARK (1995 REPRINT)

ROUGHING IT

UNIVERSITY OF CALIFORNIA PRESS

BERKLEY, CA

853 PAGES

WASSON, JOS. (1878)

BODIE AND ESMERALDA

SPAULDING, BARTO CO.

SAN FRANCISCO, CA

62 PAGES

WATSON, AMES

& BRODIE, DOUG (2002)

BIG BAD BODIE: HIGH SIERRA GHOST TOWN.

ROBERT D. REED PUBLISHERS

SAN FRANCISCO, CA

193 PAGES

WEDERTZ, FRANK S. (1969)

BODIE 1859-1900.

COMMUNITY PRINTING

AND PUBLISHING

BISHOP, CA

212 PAGES

WEHREY, JANE (2006)

VOICES FROM THIS LONG BROWN LAND: ORAL RECOLLECTIONS OF OWENS VALLEY LIVES AND MANZANAR PASTS.

PALGRAVE MACMILLAN

NEW YORK, NY

238 PAGES

WHITNEY, MARGE (1982)

MAGGIE : HER STRUGGLE FOR SURVIVAL IN OWENS VALLEY.

CHALFANT PRESS

BISHOP, CA

88 PAGES

WILLIAMS III, GEORGE (1987)

MARK TWAIN: HIS ADVENTURES AT AURORA AND MONO LAKE.

TREE BY THE RIVER PUBLISHING

DAYTON, NEVADA

93 PAGES

WILLIAMS III, GEORGE (1981)

THE GUIDE TO BODIE AND THE EASTERN SIERRA HISTORIC SITES

TREE BY THE RIVER PUBLISHING

DAYTON, NEVADA

70 PAGES

WILLIAMS III, GEORGE (1979)

ROSA MAY: THE SEARCH FOR A MINING CAMP LEGEND.

TREE BY THE RIVER PUBLSHING

CARSON CITY, NEVADA

202 PAGES

WORREL, ESTELLE ANSLEY (1980)

CHILDREN'S COSTUME IN AMERICA 1607-1910

CHARLES SCRIBER'S SONS

USA

200 PAGES

*N*ewspapers

Weekly Standard News

Mono County, Bodie

Title varies: Bodie Standard, Bodie Weekly Standard.

Microfilm: 1877(Nov7-Dec26,1878 (Jan 2-Mar 13,Apr3,17-Dec11,25) 1879(Jan4,18-Apr 5),1880 (Sept 4-Oct 9).

Daily Free Press

Mono County, Bodie

Microfilm: 1879 (Nov.3-4, 6-15,19-24,26,-Dec 13,16-6,9-30), 1880 (Jan2, 5-22,24-Feb 10,12-Mar 5,7-25,28-31,-Apr 2-9,11,14-16,18-24,28-May 27,29),1880 (June 1-10,12-17,19-25,30,-July 14,16-17,20-22-Nov 25,27-30,-Dec 2-31),1881 (July 1-Nov 23,26-Dec 31).

Bridgeport/ Bodie Chronicle Union

Mono County, Bodie and Bridgeport

Microfilmed from originals in the possession of Mr. Frank Wedertz, San Mateo, CA.

1877 (Dec 15, 1878 (Apr 13, Dec 7,21), 1879 (Jan 4,18,Mar 1, May 17, June 7, 28) 1880 (Feb 28)

Periodicals

Mono County Historical Society

2007 Newsletter :

Cain was Able. Kent Stoddard

Made in the USA
Charleston, SC
17 March 2012